WORK FOR MONEY, DESIGN FOR LOVE

Answers to the Most Frequently Asked Questions About Starting and Running a Successful Design Business

By David Airey

Work for Money, Design for Love

Answers to the Most Frequently Asked Questions About Starting
and Running a Successful Design Business

David Airey

New Riders

Find us on the Web at www.newriders.com.
To report errors, please send a note to errata@peachpit.com.
New Riders is an imprint of Peachpit, a division of Pearson Education.

Acquisitions Editor: Nikki Echler McDonald
Production Editor: Becky Winter
Development Editor: Cathy Lane
Proofer: Elaine Merrill
Indexer: FireCrystal Communications
Interior and Cover Design: David Airey
Composition: Kim Scott, Bumpy Design

ISBN-13: 978-0-321-84427-9
ISBN-10:   0-321-84427-0

9 8 7 6 5 4 3 2 1

Printed and bound in the United States of America

To everyone who has ever visited my websites, given feedback on my designs, sent a kind email, or offered encouragement.

To Cathy, Nikki, and everyone else behind the scenes for your hard work bringing this book to life.

To the contributors, for your kindness and generosity.

To my parents, for the love and support you always give.

To my wife, for choosing me back.

To you, for reading.

Contents

Introduction

This is the book I wanted to read when I became a self-employed graphic designer. It's the advice I'd give my younger self—teachings that would've put me years ahead of where I am now.

Initially, the idea was to cover everything I know about the business of design, but it serves you better if I focus solely on the most important topics—the topics made obvious through the hundreds of questions I'm regularly asked by readers of my websites.

But it's not just me offering advice. These pages also contain a wealth of knowledge contributed by vastly experienced designers all over the world, designers with hundreds of years of combined business acumen.

Becoming self-employed was the best business decision I ever made, and this book was created to help make your decision just as beneficial. So here's to all the success you're going to achieve, and all the fantastic times you're going to have along the way.

It's a pleasure to have you here.

Section I

WHERE DO YOU START?

As a child, I grew up wanting to be a soldier. Then it was a policeman, a firefighter, a footballer, an electrician, and an architect before, finally, in my mid-teens, I decided I wanted to be a designer.

Perhaps you followed a similar approach, or perhaps you took a longer or shorter route to join the design profession. Regardless, your path has led you here, to this book, ready to run your own company and make it the best it can be.

In this section, I will talk about the kind of person who dedicates a life to the business of design, as well as about the focus you need to have in order to achieve the success I know you can. And although I have absolutely no regrets about forming my company of one, I'll share why sometimes finding success isn't a walk in the park.

Chapter 1

ESSENTIAL TRAITS

There are a number of characteristics that all good design business owners share, and it's important to remind ourselves of them from time to time.

Be curious

One of humanity's greatest strengths is the desire to question. How does that work? Where did it come from? Why does it work that way? When was it invented? By questioning everything, we keep our minds active. Think of it as training—our minds are like muscles, and the more active they are, the stronger they become. The stronger they are, the greater the advantage you'll have over other design business owners.

You and I were once the best in the world at asking questions—when we were kids. But we got older, we learned to mind our own business, and we lost a lot of interest in what happens around us.

You need to reawaken that interest, let it flourish, because the desire to question is vital when dealing with your clients. Good design fulfills a brief, and without asking the right questions (we'll come to those in chapter 15), the brief won't be suitable. The project will fail. You won't delight.

One of my earliest projects in self-employment was to create an identity for a new English-themed bar and restaurant called Caramel. If I had asked more questions before starting the design work, I could've narrowed the focus to one or two brilliant ideas. But I wasn't curious enough about my client's specific design needs and about the audience she was targeting, and ultimately, neither of us was on board with the direction that needed to be taken. Because of my lack of curiosity, the client was left with too many unsuitable designs, and I was left without the second 50 percent of my fee.

Curiosity can also save you time and trouble in other ways. As a rule, I try to never fully accept anything as the truth until I've found out for myself if it is correct. I might have 99 percent confidence in my knowledge, but I always consider that remaining one percent, especially when talking to those with a difference of opinion.

A case in point: In 2009, a young designer named Jon Engle spread the news on his website that he was being sued for $18,000 by a stock agency for "stealing his own work." His news quickly resulted in a #savejon hash-tag campaign on Twitter that spread like wildfire. Jon's website crashed after his story hit the front page of Digg, and designers everywhere donated money to a legal aid fund that had been set up. But as the story emerged, the evidence suggested that he had indeed infringed upon the company's copyright. Jon ultimately apologized to everyone via Twitter in the hope of making an honest restart, but not before thousands of designers around the world had rallied to his aid without first asking for both sides of the story. There are always two sides: Search them out.

Show empathy

When someone's rude, unhelpful, or ignorant, there's a reason. Before you judge, put yourself in the shoes of the other person. There are thousands of rational reasons why someone might be feeling off center.

The same applies when dealing with clients. Your projects won't always run smoothly. Your clients won't always treat you with the respect you deserve. This is part of business, and is something you need to accept.

An excellent example: After working for a month with a client from the United States, the emails he sent me became short, abrupt, and some might say, rude. It wasn't until a few weeks later that I discovered his wife was very ill, and he was under a great deal of stress. That explained his attitude change in an instant. When this happens, remember there's a good chance that whatever is amiss is not your fault, and don't be afraid to ask your client if everything's OK.

Have confidence

Being confident isn't the same as being outgoing. It's OK to be an introvert. Confidence means believing in yourself. If you don't believe that what you have to offer is of any value, well, no one's going to pay for it.

You need to build the confidence required to sell your skills. Without it, you won't have a business. Until you've built a solid client base, *you* are your best salesperson. No one else is going to do it for you.

I once worked in telesales for *The Scotsman*, Scotland's national newspaper, selling classified ads in travel supplements. I quickly learned that unless I saw the benefit in what I was selling, I'd never make a sale. During my training and on the mock phone calls, I wasn't highlighting the benefit for the customer—namely, increased occupancy for her hotel. I needed to have confidence that people look to travel supplements when planning their holidays, and that I was calling hotel owners in an honest effort to help. Once I believed that and could convey that belief, my sales conversion rate rose to approximately 25 percent, and I ended the first day with the number of successful calls in double digits.

Don't let ten, a hundred, or a thousand "no's" put you off, because another thing I learned was that the more you practice selling, the better you become, and without those rejections, you'll never find your most-valued customers.

Truth is, you get a lot of "no's." More often than not, the design inquiries I receive from potential clients don't result in a working agreement. Why? Basically, we're not always a good fit. The client tells me their budget won't stretch, or they want to take a lead role in the actual design work, or the project deadline won't accommodate the time I need, or one of dozens of other reasons. Sometimes I catch a red flag that puts me off doing business (more on red flags in chapter 14). But every time someone says "no," I become more and more familiar with the objections raised and learn how to over-come them. If cost is prohibitive, the emphasis is shifted to how much my work can help boost client profits. If the time needed to complete the project is longer than expected, I reiterate how long solid design work lasts, and how it's better to get it right the first time.

You're the manager

We start learning management skills from a fairly early age. You manage your time, your money, your day-to-day living. But when it comes to running a business, you need to step it up. Now you're managing clients, with their budgets, deadlines, and expectations. And every client is different. Get it wrong, and you lose out.

I was managing a Nigerian client on an identity design project when, after creating a wordmark, I agreed to design and supply the artwork for corporate stationery at no extra charge. Having sent the print-ready files, I was asked to change the contact details (address, phone numbers, etc.) on two different occasions—details that should have been correct the first time around. Some weeks later, I was asked to create additional business card files for two new employees. When I responded with an invoice for my absolute minimum charge, my client wanted me to work for less than half that price. I refused, explaining that it was unsustainable to do so, but that I understood how I had placed myself in this awkward scenario by having given my work away for free.

I never heard from that client again.

The lesson? When you give a client something for free, you send the signal that everything will be free (or at least hugely discounted). And that's bad management.

Motivate yourself

When my wife has a day off work, her morning is usually spent lying in. So during the short winter days, when it doesn't get bright until around 9 a.m., when the house is a lot colder than normal, and with no boss waiting for me at the office by a set time, it takes a good deal of discipline to pull myself out of a warm bed.

What helps make it worthwhile are the wonderful emails I receive from aspiring designers all around the world. Barely a day goes by when I don't receive at least one, telling me how my blogs or my book *Logo Design Love* (New Riders, 2010) have helped them through their studies or given them the confidence to work at what they love. I don't say this to boast. I am telling you this because it is a huge source of motivation for me. You need to look for what consistently inspires you. (We'll take a more detailed look at setting up your blog in chapter 10, and at writing a book in chapter 20.)

Another motivational tool I use is the life into which I was born. I have two loving parents who remained together for 30-plus years to provide a stable home life for me, my brother, and my sister. I always had a roof over my head. I was never left hungry. I was afforded a great education through primary school, secondary school, college, and university. My family has always been supportive about what I want to do.

Too few children have these same luxuries. I owe it to my family to make the most of my time here, and I owe it to my future children—if I'm fortunate enough to have any—to provide them with the opportunities I was given.

Professionalism

It's called the design *profession* because it's full of design *professionals*. So you'd assume that acting in a professional manner was the obvious path. However, time and time again, I see fellow professionals failing to act professionally; for instance, masking their portfolio work with all the latest Web bells and whistles, or showing artwork without any context or description.

Look at how the most well-known, well-respected design studios present themselves. Chermayeff & Geismar, Moving Brands, Pentagram, Wolff Olins, Landor, Turner Duckworth, venturethree, SomeOne, johnson banks. Their websites are easy to navigate, they make it easy to contact them, and the focus is strongly on their client work, shown in context.

The copy on your website, the way you answer the phone, the time it takes you to reply to emails, the way you dress—even if you work from home, alone—these and a hundred other little details all added together are what make all the difference. Think of it like a healthy marriage—you fill the years with endless little loving gestures, rather than a single, big, dramatic event surrounded by years of disappointments.

Dublin-based designer Con Kennedy received a phone call out of the blue from a potential client asking him to "throw a few ideas together." Con replied by saying that he didn't throw ideas together, but that he'd supply a written document outlining his proposed solution with a breakdown of the costs. The very next day he received a call telling him the proposal was very professional. The client is now Con's most loyal, supplying him with work that has included storyboarding his first TV ad, regular commissions for front-end user interface design for websites, exhibition and tradeshow design, and iPhone app design. Acting professionally pays off.

Balance

Your working hours are going to increase, but your interest levels will skyrocket. That's the trade-off when you become self-employed.

It's worth it.

Trust me.

The word "work" has a certain stigma attached to it. But designers are more fortunate than most. We love what we do. To us, our job seems head and shoulders above long shifts in a hot kitchen, or walking the mean streets late at night keeping the peace. But there are chefs and police officers who love their professions, too. When you love what you do, it's not like work.

That's fantastic, but when we're that happy, soon sleep is treated as an interruption and our loved ones are given a back seat in our lives.

That's where balance is vital.

What's a good trade-off to you might be a bad one to someone else. In the words of John Maeda, president of Rhode Island School of Design, "Balance isn't about achieving 50/50. It's about oscillating around a desired norm—knowing that results may vary."

Stefan Sagmeister is one designer putting balance into practice. Every seven years he closes his New York studio and takes a year-long sabbatical. Think of it as if he intersperses his life with the retirement years he's due, except he's younger and more mobile now, and can use his sabbatical experiences to feed his upcoming work.

For me, it's hard to beat playing football with my friends each week. Fresh air. Exercise. Competition. Banter. Scoring goals.

Don't blindly trust your experience

Experience dominates our thought process. That's why children have such vivid imaginations—they're inexperienced. If you can free yourself from what you've done before, you open up a world of possibility.

At the 2011 Design Indaba in the Cape Town International Convention Centre, Michael Wolff, cofounder of Wolff Olins, spoke about how to exercise your idea-creating capacity by first getting rid of your ideas. "I mistrust my experience in terms of using my imagination; it's going to miscolor it, try to dominate it."

To quote American graphic designer Bob Gill, "A designer who knows what a solution should look like, before he knows the problem, is as ridiculous as a mathematician who knows the answer is 112 before he knows the question."

When I accept a fresh project, I treat it like a new learning experience by first researching the basics of my client's business. I look at the simplest ways in which a profit is made and the simplest goals of the business. What I don't do is consider implementing unused designs from previous client projects. There are an increasing number of websites springing up that aim to make a profit off of designers selling their unused ideas. It's a case of designers wanting to be paid twice (first by their original client, then by a never-to-be-seen client picking design off a shelf), and the client looking for previously rejected ideas. Hardly inspirational.

Don't forget to...

...smile. It's difficult to argue with the ways of the ancient Chinese. There's a particular proverb that's worth pinning to your wall:

"A man without a smiling face must not open a shop."

Good advice.

When clients initially approach me, it's mainly via email after reading my blog or viewing my online portfolio. Most of my clients have never seen me face to face. They've never talked to me on the phone. They're sending a message into the void with the aim of spending a significant amount of money to hire me. Put yourself in their shoes. You'd be a little nervous, apprehensive, unsure—especially if it was your first time working with a designer.

A new client will often email back and forth with me a bit to gauge if we're a good fit, and the next step is usually talking on the phone.

When you lift your cheek muscles and smile, the soft palate at the back of your mouth raises and makes the sound waves more fluid. The result is that your voice sounds warmer and more friendly, exactly the impression you want to give to a potential client. Conversely, when you frown, your voice sounds colder and more harsh.

Smiling works and it costs nothing; I've won thousands of dollars worth of business after talking on the phone, wearing a smile that the client can't see, but can hear.

Chapter 2

NEVER STOP LEARNING

Design school most certainly does not teach you everything. That's why you, as a successful designer, must be a lifelong learner.

The never-ending lesson

I've a picture in my mind where I'm continually learning. It's a picture in which I'm old and gray haired, yet still fascinated by design. I'm still learning new things that keep my fascination alive.

Designers are lucky: We get to learn for a living. Being lifelong learners not only benefits us personally; it's crucial to properly serving our clients.

For example, imagine you have landed a brand identity project for a cancer charity. To do the best you possibly can on the project, you need to learn about cancer; about the specific kind of cancer your client addresses; about the people who contract the disease, their demographics, their lifestyles, their worries, and their wishes; about treatments and symptoms; about the doctors and nurses who treat people with cancer; about where and how treatment takes place; about the science behind the disease and the search for a cure; about the people who work within the charity; about nonprofit organizations and how such charities need to appear to their audiences; about boards of directors and others who have responsibility for making decisions; and likely much, much more.

And that's for one little project on which you might spend only a few months. That's exciting, but scary, too.

We can't be expected to become experts overnight, regardless of the client or how much the particular business stokes our passion to learn. So we must also soak up all we can along the way, from project to project, from documentary to documentary, from news article to news article. And we take on lots of additional research beyond that.

The willingness to continually accumulate knowledge has benefits over time: The most highly remunerated design professionals are generally those who have amassed the most experience, because they have the most knowledge to draw upon for every new project, and because the more they know about life, the stronger their capacity to produce stunning work.

What design school didn't teach you

Part of being a lifelong learner is discovering more about yourself and your profession. Unfortunately, design school often neglects these areas.

I sent out a call to design graduates about what they wished was included in their courses of study. Here are the most important and frequently repeated topics, along with some views of my own.

Communicate effectively

"Design school teaches you how to talk to other designers. There needs to be an entire course on talking to people who are not designers."

— Stephen Lee Ogden

The majority of clients won't understand the technical design terms you've become familiar with. Avoid jargon. Talk to your clients like you're explaining the process to a friend (who's not a designer, obviously). In chapter 15, we'll look in more detail at specific ways to become a better communicator with clients.

> *"I'd love a class that teaches how to be diplomatic with people who don't know anything about design but think they do."*
>
> — **Emily Doliner**

You'll meet this client again and again. Many of the people you deal with will see a design meeting as the fun part of their week. They'll be keen to get involved, which is great. But you need to be clear that when it comes to design and the specific decisions you made when preparing an outcome, you're the design expert. If a client says, "Can I see it in blue?" it's your job to ask, "Why?" It's not good enough if blue is a favorite color. It must address the design brief.

> *"If you don't know how to interact with clients, or even close a sale, your talents are going to be restricted. No clients = no designing."*
>
> — **Alan Anderson**

You can learn how to sell. The best way is through trial and error. Practice is essential. You're no longer *only* a designer. You'll have a wardrobe full of different hats, some of which are mentioned in chapter 4.

Embrace all disciplines

"First-year students should be put through a rigorous program of calculus, economics, history, composition, and public speaking. The goal would be to produce first a thinker, a professional, a businessperson, and an educated individual. Only then should traditional design training begin."

— **Prescott Perez-Fox**

As stated earlier in this chapter, the most accomplished and well-paid designers are those with the most experience, those who have put in their 10,000 hours and more. If the items that Prescott mentions here were not part of your formal training, it may be well worth your time to take them on yourself.

Ask the right questions

"At least one design class should pair each student with a business seeking a new visual identity, with the students then taught how to ask intelligent questions, prompting the business to reveal its vision for the new look."

— **Jennifer Null**

The specific questions you ask your clients can make or break a project. It's also not enough to know what questions to ask. You need to know why you're asking them. Remember, be curious. Chapter 15 covers the client questions necessary for creating an effective design brief.

Learn to listen

"It's important to learn the difference between a gorgeous solution and an effective one."

— Catrina Dulay

It's not always easy to prepare for those times when a client doesn't want to use the design you've fallen in love with. It *is* easy to keep in mind that clients do know what their own customers prefer, and there are tons of instances when client feedback has greatly improved the outcome of design projects. I'll share some examples in chapter 18.

Learn to manage your time

"Prepare for the inevitable—the small projects that take time away from the major projects."

— Andrea Williams

When you're self-employed, time management takes on huge importance. You'll be working with more than one client at a time (but not so many that it adversely affects the quality of the results), and there will be times when a deadline changes, a new deliverable is required immediately, a website goes down, or advice is sought. You never know when the next client request will land in your inbox, and if you've not prepared for the hours or days it takes to address the concern, it can all be time/money down the drain. Your previously agreed-upon terms and conditions need to compensate you for such additional work. We'll look at contracts in depth in chapter 17.

Find your confident self

"I feel like certain clients abuse designers. There needs to be a class to learn how to deal with them."

— *Victor Zuniga*

Confidence in your ability as a designer enables you to stand up for your right to be paid. There will undoubtedly be people who expect you to work for next to nothing, but the more you decline these jobs, the happier you'll be, because eventually you'll be working only with those who do value your time.

If you have an opportunity to speak in front of a group, take it. With practice, you'll increase your self-confidence, which will help when dealing with potential clients. In chapter 15 we'll look at handling the client approach, and in chapter 18 we'll focus on how to best present your designs.

I used to work as an English teacher, and the experience of presenting language ideas to a class of students has helped immeasurably when it comes to presenting design ideas to a client committee. I'm better at articulating my thoughts, I don't fill any silences with "ums" and "ems," and I handle my nerves when the pressure to deliver is on. I wasn't always as calm, though. It's only with practice that I became better.

Know your business

"My course was outstanding at teaching us design, but lacked in teaching us how to run our own business."

— *Tim Daff*

I hear this over and over, and the lack of knowledge about topics such as what to charge (see chapter 16) and protecting yourself with terms and conditions (see chapter 17) are some of the main reasons for this book.

"I would make sure that all students understand the importance of print-ready files. This was an area that was barely touched upon in my courses, both BA and MA. A lot of people left the course not knowing how CMYK made a full color. Ridiculous."

— **Maria Stevens**

It wasn't until I was employed in design that I learned about prepress file requirements. It's basic information that can save you time and save your clients money.

"I would include some sort of discussion or lecture on pricing."

— **Eric Lawson**

A blog post about pricing is one that always generates discussion. Why? Because it's so bloody difficult. A class titled "Accounting for designers" sounds like one I would have skipped at university, but change the name to "How to get clients to pay what you're worth" and no one would miss it. How do we know that what we're charging is right? We sell a service based upon our education, our skill, our experience. No one's background is exactly like yours. No one can tell you if you're right or wrong. They can only tell you what they think. I've devoted a good chunk of the book toward helping you with pricing and scheduling (see chapter 16).

"The cornerstone would be where students create a product/company of their own and take it from nothing to launch, writing design and marketing briefs, and designing several key items such as an identity package, advertising, catalogs, and packaging, with the instructor acting as an art director in a design firm."

— **Jon Liebold**

The sooner we start thinking as if we're in business for ourselves, the easier it becomes to turn our actions into tangible benefits. For instance, and in hindsight, if I had started my website when I was in school instead of five years later when I became self-employed, search engines would assign a greater deal of trust to my domain name, helping with search engine rankings today. If your personal name is available as a dot com address, buy it now. Don't wait. Even if you won't trade under your personal name, it'll prove useful at some stage. Trust me. Do it now.

Other ways to keep learning

It can be easy to think you're isolated in self-employment, especially if, like me, you work from home in a one-person studio. But there's a thriving community offering design events every day—if not in your area, certainly online. Consider these ideas:

- Set aside 15 minutes each day to catch up on design-related blogs. It's as easy as opening Google Reader (or a feed reader of your choice), which in seconds has you learning from the experiences of seasoned design practitioners.

- Once a month, arrange a short tour of a local design studio. Not only will you build your network of design contacts, but you'll also learn how similar businesses operate. When contacting studio owners, always remember the question they'll be asking themselves: "What's in it for me?" That's where your own blog comes into play. Offer free promotion of the studio to your website readers. Perhaps you could prepare a few business-related questions and make an interview out of your blog feature—you pick up business tips and build your contact list, and the studio gets free promotion.

- Organize a regular coffee morning or beer evening with designers and business owners in your area. It's very likely you can work together or trade services for mutual benefit. At the same time, you can share war stories and learn from the mistakes of others, hopefully before making those mistakes yourself.

- Approach an experienced and respected designer in the hope that he or she will become your mentor. This is a huge responsibility for the person you contact, so be sure to state how many hours you expect to be devoted to you, over what period of time, and what you can do in return, such as the publishing of what you learn from your mentor on your blog (don't make this sound like a huge benefit for your mentor, because it won't be, especially as there's an added benefit for you—it'll help build your blog's readership).

- Give a design presentation or hold a workshop in a nearby college. Some people say you can learn more from your students than they can from you. I disagree. But you can become inspired by their energy, enthusiasm, imagination, and the occasional fresh idea. You can be sure your own energy and passion will sometimes wane on your journey. That's normal. Knowing how to pick them back up is what will make you great.

Chapter 3

FIND
YOUR
NICHE

The phrase, "Jack of all trades, master of none" is a little clichéd, but there's a reason why it's so common.

On the whole, it's absolutely true.

There's bound to be exceptions, if you look hard enough. But in the most extreme examples, when do you hear of an Oscar-winning actress also collecting gold at the Olympics, or a Formula One world champion winning a Pulitzer Prize for journalism?

You don't.

It's the same in business. The companies that gain the most respect are the ones that focus on just one thing, and do it extremely well.

To be the best, put all your focus, desire, passion, and commitment toward a single goal. Don't stray until you achieve what you set out to do.

Your goal might change along the way, but if you don't have a goal, you'll never score. When I launched my first design blog in 2006, I set a goal of reaching 1,000 subscribers. As soon as I reached 1,000, I moved the goalposts to 10,000. When that milestone was achieved, I made it 20,000, then 50,000, and today I have more than 150,000 subscribers, as well as two newer blogs with tens of thousands more. (There's more info on the importance of a blog in chapter 10.)

What's a niche?

A niche is a distinct segment of a market. In your case, this involves selling a specific kind of design, or targeting a specific type of client.

All it takes is a little browsing of job boards to realize the array of design-based roles that are available.

- Graphic designer
- Web designer
- Web developer
- Product designer
- Digital designer
- Magazine designer
- Packaging designer
- Brand identity designer

That's not to mention the illustrators and animators involved in the profession, and the terms that offer some overlap, such as "user experience," "front-end," "operator," or "artworker."

It can be confusing, but narrowing down what best suits you is as easy as simply doing what you love. What do you most enjoy about design? Is it print? Web? Brand identity? Motion graphics? Something else? Only you know what gives you the most enjoyment.

Choose to spend your energy on what you love, and once you narrow your outlook, that's when you'll find yourself on the path to becoming truly great.

You can further define your niche (and thereby eliminate some of your competition) by targeting a specific type of client or sector.

Here are a few possibilities, each of which is highly focused:

- Designing websites for restaurants
- Working exclusively with hair salons

- Doing brand identity design for small to medium-sized enterprises
- Creating websites that are easily customized by the client
- Working solely with photographers
- Focusing on car garages
- Specializing in stationery design
- Devoting your design to the fashion industry
- Working with real estate businesses
- Designing for companies with a strong ethical stance
- Even creating a niche position donating 10 percent of your client fee to a specific charity, perhaps even a charity of your client's choice, in their locale.

Remember, though, the narrower your niche, the fewer people there'll be to make up your client base. So get specific, but not *too* specific. It's yet another balancing act you need to perform during the course of self-employment.

Why specialize?

There are millions of designers, all competing for design clients. By placing yourself inside a specific design niche, you decrease the number of competitors and give yourself a greater chance of being the go-to name for the service you provide.

Think about it. If you get 100 clients over 10 years, and if each of those 100 projects result in the same deliverable, such as a brand identity package, an e-commerce website, or a book cover illustration, you're training yourself to be a specialist—the person everyone wants to work with when it comes to that specific outcome.

On the flip side, if those 100 projects result in a range of 20 or 30 different deliverables, you're casting a wider net with the ability to offer more services, but you won't become as skilled in a specific service. As such, you won't command the premium price you're aiming for. And you won't always be doing the sort of work that you really and truly love.

Another benefit revolves around client acquisition and word-of-mouth marketing. Imagine you gain a client within the financial sector. You produce a fantastic visual identity and receive a glowing testimonial. This client will undoubtedly be meeting with countless other financial professionals, many of whom will be your potential clients. If a word-of-mouth referral leads these professionals to your website, where they see a portfolio full of projects for similar financial businesses, they're much more likely to hire you than if they see a portfolio full of work for restaurants, animal shelters, or massage therapists.

So by specializing, you increase the conversion rate when it comes to recommendations from your best salespeople—previous clients.

When you're micro-focused, the content on your website is also micro-focused. How does this help? Search engines will come to treat your online presence as a source of expert advice around the topic you specialize in. As an example, there are about 153 million search results on Google for "graphic design," but less than one million for "brand identity design." Which first-page position do you think it's easier to compete for?

Of course, you can take it too far, targeting a search engine result for something like "Wordpress theme design for dog-walking companies." So again, it's about being specific, but not narrowing your service to an extent where you can't sustain a business.

Spread the risk

Don't pigeonhole yourself with a reliance on a particularly small client pool. For example, I specialize in brand identity design. If my speciality was brand identity design for fire brigades, I could easily find myself without any work.

When I first thought about self-employment, I wanted to specialize in print design, and more specifically, flyer design for the music industry. I love music and design, and this was my way to combine the two. But it soon became apparent that this wasn't a great way to make my fortune. Music flyers can be found in practically every student's portfolio, and there's never a shortage of students on hand to design for their favorite DJs or groups. With a lack of a name for myself, the competition was too fierce for such a narrowly defined niche.

But one of the beauties of the design profession is that every industry needs your skills. Every business needs a brand identity, even if it's a simple word mark in a specific typeface. Building recognition rates around a single visual identity breeds trust among a company's audiences, and business owners appreciate the value of trusting customers.

The process of finding your niche is likely to involve some trial and error. What you love doing today might not be what you'll love doing tomorrow.

But your niche is likely to be obvious to you. You've been doing it already. You don't feel like you're working when you're doing it, and breaking for lunch sometimes seems like an unwanted interruption.

It comes down to this: Until you try in self-employment what you love doing in employment, until you focus your energy on delighting your own customers rather than those of your boss, you're never going to be in total control of your career, in total control of your earning potential.

Now is the time when all of that changes.

Chapter 4

PROS AND CONS OF SELF-EMPLOYMENT

Before I started, I knew it wasn't going to be easy. Plenty of people told me that ahead of time, most cautioning me to spend more time as an employed person before becoming self-employed.

My first serious thoughts about going it alone came when I was in employment and sustained a nasty ankle injury playing football. I took time away from the office, but could still easily get the job done from home. I realized I didn't need to be commuting to work, but my boss wasn't keen on remote staff, so I began contemplating life in a home studio. It was around a year later when I finally made the switch, serving my notice in employment, but securing my previous employer as my first retainer client.

One sort of very important advice that I neglected to seek out was talking to someone experienced in the design profession about the ups and downs of running a design business. You need to have the advice of others before you make the jump. A particular lesson I quickly learned on my own was that in order to be successful you need to really want it, because if you don't, there are a thousand others who'll step up to the plate, a thousand others who will win the clients before you can say, "What's your deadline?" My eyes weren't as open to the fact as they could've been. I'm sure more experienced designers would have helped prepare me for the workload I was letting myself in for.

But you're not talking to someone else right this minute. You're reading this book. So to give you the insights I didn't have, here are some of the pros and cons from my first seven years as an independent designer.

PRO: You set your own hours

There's no more 9–5, Monday to Friday. No more forcing yourself out of bed to make a profit for some boss. When I need time during the afternoon for a dental appointment, to visit the bank, or to simply go for a walk along the coast, I can. I don't need to ask for permission or to let someone know where I'm going. Of course, it's still essential to have a routine, and to set specific hours when your clients can reach you, but in general, you'll have a lot more flexibility when organizing your life.

CON: People expect you to work 24/7

I started working with clients all around the world in very different time zones. Taking full responsibility for every detail of a project was new to me, and I wasn't careful enough about setting boundaries. So my phone rang in the middle of the night, when I was in bed, fast asleep, and certainly not thinking about serving clients.

PRO: You set your own rates

The sky's the limit for what you decide to quote. There are no predefined income brackets that someone else places you in, and there are no annual pay reviews where you attempt to convince your superior that you're worth a place in the next bracket. As a self-employed person, it's up to you to determine what your skills are worth. That was a huge incentive for me, but it also leads to one of my biggest headaches.

CON: How do you know what to charge?

This is new territory. No one can tell you exactly what figure to show on your project quotes. No one knows your education and work history as well as you do. No one knows the attention to detail you put into each and every client project.

This is your call. Other people can help, and we'll look closely at pricing in chapter 16, but ultimately, this is your call. It's not easy.

PRO: You're doing the job you love

That's why you're in it for the long haul. You love it. Think about your friends and family, and ask yourself how many of them truly love the jobs they're doing. When I think of those close to me and how many of them work just to pay the bills and support their families, it makes me incredibly thankful for the position in which I find myself.

You also need to love your job because for everything that's great about running your own design business, it's not all roses. Your passion will get you through the hard times and through those situations when a particular project isn't everything you'd hoped it would be. But there are other situations that can test your love. Check chapter 14 for advice on what to do then.

CON: Some people think that because you love your job, you'll happily work for free

If you've not encountered this problem already, you soon will. On this very day, when I'm writing these words, I received yet another email from a potential client without a design budget. What did he offer me? A link to my portfolio at the foot of his website.

"Think of the exposure!"

It's incredibly common that people believe they can get something for nothing, regardless of the product or service they need. Thanks, but no thanks. When you have and show respect for yourself and your work, others will learn to respect what you offer.

PRO: You make the rules

This is where small businesses have a huge advantage over large organizations. If you want to start a new marketing campaign, you can do it today. There's no need for meeting after meeting to vainly attempt to predict the outcome before spending money on the idea. Go right ahead. You're in charge.

When I was beginning, I wanted to attract local clients— people I could meet face-to-face so I could build more of a relationship than I could through purely online means. So I designed my corporate stationery, got it printed at a local print shop, polished my portfolio, put on my best shoes, and hit the city center. Was it successful? Not particularly, but I was trying. I decided to cold-call market myself in person and just got out there and did it. A few days of preparation were all that was necessary. Now, imagine if the Coca-Cola Company was implementing a door-to-door marketing push. How many meetings and how many months of preparation do you think that would take?

CON: No one explains the rules

I admit that much of what I did in my early days involved flying by the seat of my pants. In hindsight, I was certainly more naïve than I would have hoped.

My first business name was New Dawn Graphics. Yes, it makes me cringe. The website was geared up to make me look like a team of design professionals rather than what my business really was—just me. I did plan to bring other people on board and to subcontract much of the work, but in those early days none of that happened, and I became increasingly uncomfortable with the generic business name.

When I finally switched the brand name to David Airey, that wasn't the end of the mistakes. I made plenty—especially with my website—and I'll tell you about the worst Web mistakes in chapter 10. (If you want to know about naming your brand, there's some excellent advice from Bernadette Jiwa in chapter 7.)

You, on the other hand, you were paying particular attention throughout your studio experience, weren't you? Maybe? If not, it is vital that you start now: Pick up as much advice as possible while in design employment—in project management, dealing with clients, bookkeeping, pricing, and so on—because the more prepared you are, the smoother the transition to self-employment will be. My cold-call, door-to-door approach, for instance—that's not the way to approach potential clients. Chapter 11 contains marketing advice that's infinitely more useful.

PRO: If you want a holiday, you take a holiday

Are your friends going away on a last-minute trip? Did some festival tickets suddenly become available? Have you been more stressed than normal lately? You no longer need to juggle your time off around your work colleagues' prebooked holidays. Your only concern is with your current clients. Treat them well. Then treat yourself. There's no boss to give you a Christmas bonus, or to tell you to have the rest of the day off. That privilege rests on your shoulders. Don't let it slip away.

Since going independent, in addition to working harder, I've seen a lot more of the world, too, spending time off in Malaysia, Spain, Russia, Thailand, the United States, India, China, Turkey, Vietnam, and many other destinations. I would never have had the time off to do so many things had I still been working in someone else's office.

CON: You don't get paid for time off

A definite downside of self-employment—you can forget about those paid holidays, paid sick days, and paid maternity/paternity leave days. Those are comforts you can no longer afford, unless you add passive income streams into your business. (Speaking of those, we'll get to some in chapter 20.)

PRO: You get to wear a lot of different hats

Design, branding, marketing, communications, project management, accounting, public relations, business management, IT, Web development—these are just a few of the many hats you need to wear. What is it people say about the spice of life?

In my days of formal education, I took a post-graduate course in management, and although I don't manage a team of employees, what I learned from that course has definitely helped me tackle the non-design side of my business. You'll need to be well-rounded, as they say.

CON: Sometimes you just want to wear your favorite hat

Rest assured that at some point you'll want to be a designer at the exact time you need to be an accountant. I've been knee-deep in the design research stage of a project right when it was time to sort out my invoices for the year and file my tax return.

The solution here, of course, is simple time management. When it comes to taxes, for instance, I've learned to get mine sorted at the end of the financial year rather than let them interfere with design time later. The point is, you can't ignore the other hats no matter how uncomfortable the fit.

PRO: Your clients come from all walks of life, all around the world

One of the best parts of my job is the amount of variety supplied by my clients. They can just as easily be halfway around the world, in a completely different culture, as they can the other side of town. In fact, given the nature of my search-engine optimization, the clients that find me through my website are actually more likely to hail from the other side of the Atlantic. (You'll find advice on boosting your own search-engine rankings in chapter 10.)

It's not just working with different people that inspires me. It's how the nature of their businesses changes with almost every project. With one project I'll be learning about surfing, in another about tequila, then in another about luxury fashion or medical advances or digital music. The topics you get to study are limited only by those clients you choose to work with, and that certainly keeps my job interesting.

CON: You probably can't meet every client in person

It's hard to beat meeting face-to-face when it comes to building relationships, so with the vast majority of my client base being overseas, I'm unlikely to create bonds as strong as they could be. This doesn't mean I can't surpass clients' expectations. It's just that I won't always be in the room to see the delight on their faces.

There's a positive in there, too, though: On many past projects, I've saved valuable time when all the process needs is a video call rather than the hours I would have spent traveling to and from face-to-face meetings.

PRO: The 10-meter commute from bedroom to home studio

Not having to climb into a freezing cold car each winter morning and battle the rush-hour traffic to get to work, as well as paying for gas and parking, are all great reminders of why I chose self-employment. Now I save the money and time I'd normally spend commuting and use those resources to do what I want to do.

CON: The inability to leave your work "at the office"

When your workplace is where you live, it's all too easy to work incredibly long hours. When your office is meters from your living room, there's a temptation to pop back into "work" when it's more important to spend time with your family. Avoid using your laptop in bed, because it's a lot easier to get a good night's sleep when you associate your bed with sleeping—not watching TV or reading, and definitely not working. I've previously contributed to many sleepless nights by checking emails when propped up by pillows. It has quickly led to an inability to switch off, and when I've been able to get some sleep I've found myself waking up with headaches after grinding teeth through stress (or waking up with a shove from my wife when my teeth grinding has disturbed her sleep). Self-discipline is essential.

PRO: Taking your laptop outdoors

The sun's shining, there's blue sky as far as the eye can see, and it's definitely not a day to be cooped up in the office. So leave! Get your laptop and head to the park, the beach, the countryside, a beer garden. Or, remember what I said about holidays and taking the afternoon off? Feel free to leave the laptop in the office. Take your partner, instead.

CON: The weather doesn't always cooperate

I'm not even sure this is a "con." See the entry on "10-meter commute," above. Enough said.

Section II

WHO DO YOU NEED TO BE?

The hardest part is starting. Millions of great ideas come and go every day because people don't put them into action. This time it's different. This time it's you. You're starting your journey, and it's going to be brilliant.

To point you in the right direction, this section will share smart business practices and explain how to form and execute a business plan, how to brand yourself and launch your website, where your clients will come from, what legalities you need to know, and a lot more vital information, shared by seasoned professionals.

Chapter 5

WORK DIRECT OR BE A SUBCONTRACTOR?

Choices—you'll need to make thousands of them. That's something I didn't really think about at the start of my self-employment. When I was employed by someone else, the majority of corporate decisions were made by my colleagues and superiors, and I focused on decisions around print and Web management. But now, everything comes back to me, from profit-making and balancing the books to marketing drives and public relations.

One decision has to be made again and again: I can either deal directly with clients (the people buying the actual design work) or with a studio or agency (the people who have been hired by the client and who regularly subcontract design work to design specialists).

There are positives and negatives to both approaches. You can decide for yourself which works best for you.

Dealing directly with clients

For the past couple of years, all of my client projects have involved working directly with the organization buying the design. It wasn't always like that. For a few years previous, there was a roughly 50/50 split, with the other half coming from agencies that subcontracted me (we'll get to the other half shortly). In recent years I've found it more to my advantage to work directly with clients. This may or may not be the same for you.

Pros

There is one enormous "pro" to this approach: When I've dealt directly with clients, I've had a lot more sway when it comes to achieving consensus on a specific design direction. There are a couple of reasons why. For a start, I'm being

hired because of *my* work, *my* reputation, and *my* approach to design—that is, not the work of an agency. Additionally, I'm also much closer to the decision maker(s), so there's a much smaller chance of ideas being lost in translation, as they might be when client feedback is relayed through an agency's account manager.

Cons

When you are working directly with the client, however, you're unlikely to be discussing the project with someone who is anywhere near as familiar with design as you are. They might have a design team within the company, but most often, the decision maker is not experienced in design.

Only a handful of my clients have been from typically creative professions. There have been a few that I've been fortunate enough to work with: Berthier, for instance, an interior design firm in Japan, and TalkTo, a unique "text any business" startup where one of the decision makers was extremely proficient in Web design and development. For me, such clients are the exception, but for you, this is going to depend on your chosen niche (we covered some niches in chapter 3). After all, maybe you'll target creative firms, such as architects or industrial designers, for your client base.

In my experience, when dealing with those who aren't so design proficient, you need to be a lot more up front about how you work and about the steps involved in the process. This is where having an informative and well-developed website can save you a ton of time. (Chapter 10 focuses on launching your online presence.)

When a potential client gets in touch, one of the first things I want to know about him or her is whether the person has already dealt with a designer on another project. This sets some of the tone I use when explaining certain stages of the project. For instance, if it's the client's first time hiring a designer, I'll be sure to reiterate that all questions, regardless of how basic they might seem, are more than welcome, because a big part of my job is to set the client's mind at ease. Discovering if this person has hired designers in the past can also highlight red flags (see chapter 14 for additional info on those).

Having worked on more than 100 brand identity projects, I'm generally asked many more questions by clients with no prior experience of identity design. Questions are necessary, for both parties (discussed further in chapter 15).

Subcontracting with agencies

It makes sense that design agencies and consultancies choose to subcontract work to independent designers. After all, every project is different, and clients will often make requests that only the largest agencies are able to cater to in-house. So after a few years in self-employment, I found myself receiving fairly regular work requests from agencies around the world— agencies who had found me through my website.

Pros

I was pleased, obviously, because it was a vote of confidence from those who deliver a creative service. When you receive such offers, be proud of your skills, and whether you choose to accept the project, be appreciative to those making the approach. You never know how much work might be sent your way by a particular agency, and as agencies are generally geared up to deal with larger projects, you can also expect more opportunities to work with well-known brands. Treat these people well.

Agencies and studios will also be better equipped to attract steadier streams of business—they need more clients than you in order to sustain the profitability of a team. So working as a subcontractor on one project can quickly lead to a succession of regular approaches from the same agency. This can significantly lessen the worries you'll have about where the next client will come from, especially when your clients are normally turned over rather than retained, as is the case in my niche of brand identity design.

Another pro when subcontracted is that you're privy to the working practices of experienced creative companies, and you can put a sharper incline on your learning curve throughout each project.

Cons

At the same time, you need to be careful when subcontracted so you know what you might be letting yourself in for. With that in mind, consider this useful passage from the website of Andy Budd, founding partner of the UK-based user experience firm Clearleft, in which he discusses the perils of working through "middlemen."

> "So many agencies win work first and then try to resource later. I'm constantly meeting freelancers that get brought into projects at the last minute and are forced to lie about their status as a freelancer. Many of these freelancers end up having to run the projects themselves with little or no support from their paymasters. So while clients buy into the seniority of the team, they end up getting none of the benefits. In many cases Web design consultancies can be little more than employment agencies, hiring people in cheaply and simply slapping a margin on their day rate.

"I was recently having a pint with a friend who informed me that out of the 200-plus people in his design and development agency, just 10 were designers and 20 were developers. To that they had a 60-person sales team, 40 project managers, 20 account handlers, and then a load of admin people. People came to this NMA top-100 agency for their expertise, when the majority of their work was actually executed by freelancers, unbeknownst to their clients, of course. The agency was little more than an admin and sales front, being fed large amounts of money and excreting mediocre design."

I've found myself in a similar situation. A New York-based agency approached me on May 1, 2007, asking if I'd create a logo for one of its clients. I was relatively inexperienced at the time and was happy with the opportunity for work, so I accepted the terms: I needed to start immediately and had until May 12 to submit preliminary ideas; I needed to work for the budget set by the agency; and I couldn't disclose to anyone that the work had been developed by me.

In hindsight, those three points would be deal breakers today. The terms were entirely set by the agency, so from the outset I was at a disadvantage.

At the time, though, I agreed to the terms on May 2, but it wasn't until May 7 when the agency was ready to provide the background details I needed, and it wasn't until May 9 when I received a down payment on my fee. The deadline for preliminary ideas hadn't changed, of course.

When ideas were ready, even though I presented the work to the agency's client through a conference call, feedback still came from my contact at the agency, as well as from the client. This meant I was getting two opinions on the work— one from the client and another from the agency. And it was awful feedback, too, such as—and I quote directly from an email—"Can we use bright or softer colors to support the message like: yellow, green, purple, and other positive and inspirational colors?" Another agency email began, "Sorry to keep annoying you with my ideas, but here's a thought…" followed not long after with another email titled, "More annoying ideas."

Don't get me wrong, it's good when a client shares ideas. But it felt as if no matter what I produced, my agency contact just wanted me to execute her ideas. I was hired for my software proficiency rather than my creativity. Then, in addition, the ideas I presented also needed to be signed off by her client.

Eventually, a conference call with the agency and client drew positive remarks all round. That was until the agency later told me the client's partner wasn't happy. I didn't know there was a partner involved; otherwise, I would have insisted he was included in the conference call. That's what happens when you don't have control of the process.

How did the project finish? On May 21, after numerous revision rounds and conference calls, the agency finally told me, "I'm not really sure what the client wants." None of the designs were used, and I didn't receive the remaining 50 percent of my fee.

When you're subcontracted, you lose a level of contact with the decision maker(s) and, in effect, need to overcome two layers of consensus (the agency, then the client). So the chances of success can be doubly difficult.

I don't mean to put a damper on the importance of client feedback. More often than not, it's going to be invaluable to the success of the project, and we'll look at some examples of how to use it more successfully in chapter 18.

Chapter 6

PLANNING FOR SUCCESS

The late French writer and aviator Antoine de Saint-Exupery once said, "A goal without a plan is just a wish." In order to succeed in your new business, you need a plan, something that outlines your route, the resources you will need, and everything you hope to experience along the way. You need a business plan.

A business plan is both a touchstone and an aspirational document. By consulting it frequently, you will be able to keep track of where you are going and know if you are making progress. Additionally, if you need a business loan to help kick-start your venture, the business plan will be the foundation on which your bank manager (hopefully) approves the loan.

The plan will change along the way to meet fluctuations in the market and changes in your life. The first iteration of my plan said absolutely nothing about blogs and about how they'd prove to be the cornerstone of my business. (I wish it had, though; if I had planned to launch a blog from the very beginning, I'd be a year ahead of myself in terms of progress.).

Of course, the best-laid plans can come unstuck, and they sometimes will (see chapter 14 for instances of firing the client, to name just one dilemma), but it's the formation of these plans that greatly aids a project's success rate. They will help get you back on track. And just like when you study a map before driving across the country, you're less anxious and you get there quicker, with fewer dead ends and less wasted energy.

Your business plan is a comprehensive document that contains information about your marketplace; what your definition of success is (what personal income you would like to earn, for instance, or the date by which you can hire an employee); what to do when Plan A fails; your financial

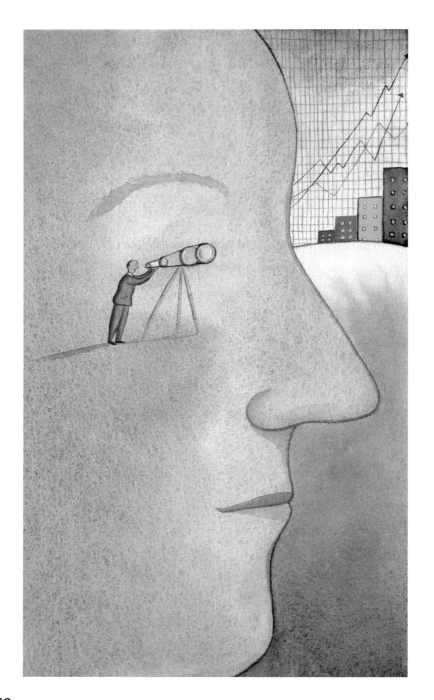

projections; and anything else relevant to your business. It's a fluid document you can update when situations change, but do keep the original intact so in the future you can look back to see how far you've come. Obviously, if you're using the document for outside investment in your business, it'll need to look the part, but you're a designer—that should come easy. However, do have at least one other person check it for typos.

There are entire books and software packages that can help you generate an effective business plan, and it would be wise to consult one. What I'd like to offer here is how to tailor a plan to fit an independent designer like yourself. Marketing guru and blogger Seth Godin offers particularly good advice. In one of his posts, from May 2010, he recommends five distinct sections in your business plan: truth, assertions, money, alternatives, and people. I'd suggest keeping the sections in this order.

Truth

Here's where you cover everything you know about the state of the design profession: about why there's a demand for your skill, about those who are succeeding, about those who have failed (and why). It's where you show how much you understand about the business you're getting into.

A sample fact (please note that these are just examples; don't base your business decisions on them): You might say that 56 percent of respondents to the "2011 Design Industry Voices" survey (conducted by the Institute for Public Policy Research) were intending to leave their agency; that 35 percent had been in their job less than a year; and that in the next 12 months 58 percent were intending to change their employer. With such a high staffing turnover and with a scarcity of jobs in the current economic climate, there will likely be more designers entering self-employment, and therefore greater competition for you. These facts might also affect your ability to retain your best employees should you choose to expand.

You might follow up with information like this: Rachel Fairley, lead author of the "Design Industry Voices" report and managing director at Fairley & Associates noted, "Over half (58 percent) of respondents told us their agency is employing less permanent staff, and 55 percent that they are using more freelancers." So although there is likely more competition between independent designers competing for clients, the flip side is that it opens up new avenues to be subcontracted by agencies.

You might also talk about how the design profession has exploded during the past few decades, partly due to the decreasing expense of hardware and software, as well as the expansion of the Internet and the ability to work from any location with an Internet connection.

This section doesn't express an opinion. It simply states things as they are, in as much detail as is necessary. The point of the section is to be clear to yourself (and to potential investors) that you know how the design business works. You can include spreadsheets, reports, surveys, market analyses—whatever it takes to paint an accurate picture.

Assertions

This is your plan A, what you want to happen. You're getting into business because you want to do something. You want to do X and Y is going to happen. Here's where you detail the steps you'll take and what you hope to achieve.

Talk about the niche you're targeting (see chapter 3), about how much of your earnings will come from working directly with clients and how much from being subcontracted (see chapter 5), about how you're going to brand yourself to stand out from your competitors (see chapters 7 and 8), and about what you'll do to attract and retain clients (see chapters 10 and 11).

To give you an idea of what this section might be like, I've created a sample that I might use for myself, given the experience I've already amassed, if I was starting my business today.

I am David Airey, a Northern Ireland-based graphic designer. I will focus on creating brand identities for established companies. My target client is a medium- to large-size company that has been established for more than ten years. The client has been growing steadily but has been working with an outdated visual identity and is in need of a new design to reach the next level and to bring all departments together with cohesive visuals.

I will operate as a sole proprietorship from my home-based studio in County Down, Northern Ireland, and will grow to profitability by month ten.

My company's primary goal is to boost clients' profits by creating brand identities that help attract and retain the ideal customer base. Although measuring this is not an exact science, client profits will be recorded for three years either side of the identity relaunch.

Clients will fall into two distinct groups: medium-size companies that are typically 15 to 50 employees, and large-size companies of 50+ employees.

Clients will be attracted through my strong online presence, through referrals from 100+ previous design clients, through a highly targeted and tailored self-promotional mailing delivered to companies I aspire to work with, and through my knowledge of search-engine optimization coupled with highly visible websites. One aspect of my websites that helps set them apart from others is the focus and in-depth featuring of the process within brand identity design projects.

The first client account will be established by the end of month one, with three further accounts secured by the end of the second quarter. The first year will bring eight new client accounts.

Money

Let's look at some of the costs I'd incur if starting anew:

- Office furniture, including a large desk, a desk lamp, an ergonomic chair, a large bookshelf, a filing cabinet, a sofa, and a coffee table.

- A 27-inch iMac, a MacBook Air, an A3-size color printer, and the following software: Adobe Creative Suite, font management utilities, Microsoft Office, iWork.

- Development of my online portfolio, which will include my own design and development time.

- Utilities, including gas, electricity, telephone, and Internet.

- Assorted office supplies.

- Business stationery, which includes design time by me, and third-party print costs.
- An up-to-date library of creative magazines, journals, and reference books.

I'd go on to mention how much cash is needed in reserve to cover outgoings during quiet spells, because (as I now know) throughout my self-employment there will be months when I'm inundated with quote requests from potential clients, and then the next month will pass without a squeak.

Purchasing type fonts is an expense I hadn't considered at the beginning. I've since learned to absolve this cost into client invoices, but when my charges were much smaller than they are now, this could easily eat away at my profits. If there was a plus side, once the font license was bought, it was available for any appropriate future projects, so font purchasing could be seen as an investment of sorts.

Don't forget, earnings need to cover the more mundane expenses in life, such as office rental if needed, dental costs, car maintenance, health insurance, and so on. And it would be great if you could pay yourself a salary.

In addition, this section of the plan includes how much clients will be charged and answers questions such as: How will you accept payment? How will you spend your income? What will the balance sheet look like for the first three years? (More info on pricing and bookkeeping in chapter 16.)

Alternatives

This is your Plan B. What happens when X doesn't result in Y? What happens if your earnings plan doesn't work out as you had envisioned? What happens if you are not able to attract the sort of clients you wished for? At what point do you decide that your original plans aren't working? What do you do if a client won't pay?

You can't address every single eventuality that might befall you. But your alternatives should at the very least address every assertion that you have made earlier in your plan.

For instance, if client work dries up for a month or more, these quiet months are ideal times to proactively market yourself (see chapter 11) or to create passive income streams (see chapter 20). Add your latest projects to your portfolio so those next potential clients can see your strongest work. We all improve with time, after all, so show yourself in the best light possible.

Here's another example of when a Plan B might be needed, an actual and unfortunate incident from my life. How to promote myself is definitely part of my own business plan. A big part of that is online promotion, through my blog and website. Everything was going swimmingly: My website had been pulling in more than 2,000 unique daily visits. Not a massive amount, but for a one-man operation, 700,000 annual visitors can generate a healthy amount of new design business.

Then someone took me offline while I was away on holiday. Five days before my trip was over, I got some worrying emails from friends that told me my website had disappeared and that my domain name (www.davidairey.com) was now redirecting to a random website. I was confused and anxious.

Long story short: A Gmail flaw allowed a hacker to abduct almost my entire self-promotional plan and all of the value it had built for my business. I had no backup plan for this, especially being away from home. I called upon the close contacts I'd made within the design community to ask for help.

I received an enormous amount of support from thousands of others: Several days after my arrival home, my story was mentioned on the *New York Times* website, accumulated thousands of "thumbs ups" on Digg, was on the front page of Edinburgh's *Evening News* (I was living in Edinburgh at the time), and was blogged about on hundreds of websites. This flood of publicity prompted GoDaddy (where my domain had been transferred to by the thief) to give almost immediate help in returning the domain to my possession.

I was lucky. Very, very lucky. Like I said before, there's almost no way to predict that something so random might happen. But if my website was so valuable to me, I should have had a plan in place to either quickly replace, repair, or otherwise protect it.

A further occasion when you'll need a plan B is when you've spent many weeks crafting work for a client, and now it's time for the presentation. It flops. The client just can't see how it's going to work for his or her business, despite previously agreeing with the general idea when you did a walk-through in a face-to-face meeting. Now what? (Have a look at chapter 17 for terms and conditions that must be agreed upon prior to the designer/client working relationship.)

Or what if you're in a bad accident and can't work for six months? If it's just you taking sole responsibility for the business, how are you going to survive? So include those passive income streams from chapter 20 in your plan. They can prove vital to the long-term success of your company.

People

To be as successful as possible, you need to build and develop relationships with a host of others, and I'm not just talking about your clients.

We talked about subcontracting in chapter 5, but not the kind I'm referring to here. This is where *you* do the subcontracting, where *you* assign specific elements of a project to other creatives. Doing so has benefited me in a number of ways:

- I'm able to offer my clients a broader range of deliverables, making the client's task of outsourcing easier to handle.

- I get to focus on the creative work I do best and enjoy most.

- The elements of a project that I don't specialize in can still be completed by specialists, rather than me attempting to learn on the job, therefore keeping the quality of work to a maximum.

In this section of the plan, you'll show what kinds of specialists you're going to build relationships with, as well as how you'll do it. For instance, the comment threads on my websites have proved invaluable for developing rapport with designers and developers. When people leave comments on a blog post and add a link to their own websites, I make a point of clicking in order to learn more about them. They obviously have an interest in the creative topics I'm writing about, so there's a good chance they'll specialize in work similar to my own.

Although it might be too big of a leap for someone just starting out, it's also worth at least considering how you might expand in the future with the addition of employees. Perhaps, like me, you'll find you prefer working as a one-person company, or perhaps you're in it to grow beyond my current situation.

How long?

You're probably wondering how long your business plan should be. Deficiencies in plans are more likely to be qualitative than quantitative, but if you're searching for a business loan, and if the plan is for the benefit of investors, aim to record the necessary information in 20 to 30 pages. If it's for your eyes only, you can work with fewer.

Chapter 7

BRAND NAMING

One of the bigger mistakes I made when I struck out on my own happened in 2005 when I chose my first business name. For the duration of that year, I called myself New Dawn Graphics. In hindsight, it's terrible, but I didn't pluck it from thin air. I toiled, drew up a short list, asked friends and family and people I respected, and although New Dawn Graphics wasn't a runaway favorite, it got more thumbs ups than any of the alternatives. So I ran with it.

Of course, the people I surveyed didn't have to live with the name day in and day out. They were making a decision after just a few minutes of thinking (perhaps even seconds). I should have taken more responsibility and carried out more research and testing.

After some months, I became increasingly uncomfortable with my choice even though I'd already designed and paid for the printed stationery and website.

It was around one year before I changed my company name to David Airey. It was just me, after all, and I've not regretted the decision in the slightest.

Perth-based Bernadette Jiwa is a friend of mine who specializes in brand naming. In fact, she was the one who came up with the title for this book, *Work For Money, Design For Love*. I asked her to impart her expert advice to form the basis of this chapter. Thankfully, she obliged, because while trading under my personal name has helped me achieve more than I expected, it might not be the right move for you. Bernadette offers a wider perspective.

According to Bernadette, you have nine seconds to convince potential clients that you are The One, or at least to get them to take a second look. "The name you choose for

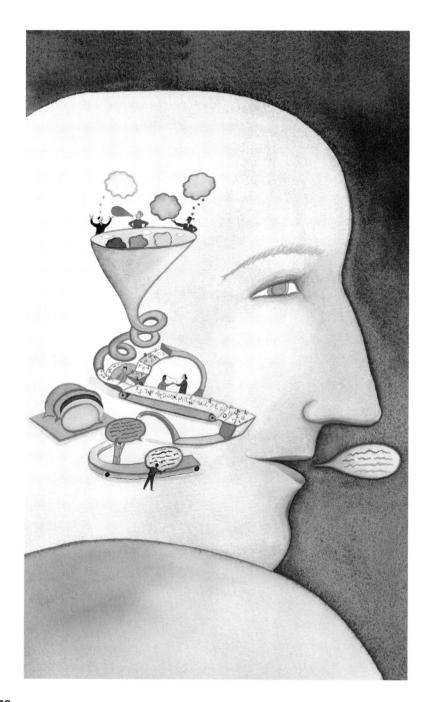

your business is not just an asset you will own forever, it is one of the most important elements of your brand strategy," she notes.

Everything begins with a name

We love a good story. We have done so since we were read to as kids, and it's the same in business. Your story is what people will buy into, and your business name is the hook on which you hang your story and start the conversation with customers.

Bernadette goes on to say, "It's more than the mechanism you give people to identify you. Your brand name is what makes that initial emotional connection with your customers, and when you earn their trust and loyalty, it's the way they spread the news about you. A great brand name doesn't just describe your business, it sets the stage, articulates your position, and conveys the unique personality of your brand."

It might be tempting to head straight to a domain registrar to see what's available, but before you do, here are the questions Bernadette recommends you ask yourself these questions.

What's my mission?
What difference do I want to make with my business? To use myself as an example, my mission is to increase the percentage of projects I work on that are for nonprofit organizations, ensuring the work I produce is for companies with ethics that align with my own.

What's my vision?
What are or will be the results and effects of my work and what my business does in the future? Again, using myself as

an example: Those companies I work with will, as a result of my services, be better equipped to meet their own ethical objectives.

What are my core values?
What are the attitudes and beliefs that shape my business culture and the things my brand stands for? Personally, I have a strong desire to help companies that help and care for others. For instance, I'd much rather work alongside Marie Curie Cancer Care, a UK charity that provides palliative care to the terminally ill in their own homes, than I would an arms manufacturer, such as BAE Systems.

What is my unique value proposition?
Don't just think about what you do, but also why you do it. Why will clients and customers want to do business with me?

Do I have an emotional selling point?
What's the intangible that I am selling? Think *feelings* not facts. Do you offer a sense of connection, freedom, ego, belonging, or anything else that will appeal to customers?

What is the essence of my brand?
What is at the core of what I do, the image it portrays and the signals it sends? The essence of my brand is that it's successful because I make it less about me and more about my clients—about the direction their companies are heading, and the success they will achieve.

Describe what you do and why you do it.
Aim to condense this into one line that communicates everything. This could eventually be a strapline if you choose to use one. For instance, I'm passionate about design, and I'm passionate about helping businesses I believe in to surpass their goals. I earn a living by combining those passions.

Who is my target audience?

Paint a picture of your ideal client. Understand as much as you can about them, their goals, aspirations, and their personal and business priorities.

What's my brand identity?

How does the consumer perceive my brand? What words might they use to describe it? What words would I want them to use?

What type of name do I want to consider?

Am I building a personal brand? Do I want an evocative, descriptive, invented, or other name?

Once you can answer all of these questions and have a short list of names, there are practicalities to consider.

Domain availability

There's a certain weight attached to owning and operating with a .com domain extension, but if the .com name isn't available, or if it's already in use by a brand in a different industry, consider using your country extension .us, .co.uk, .in, and so on.

A .com extension is great, but it's not the be-all and end-all. Take the United States-based company Instagram, for example. In 2012, the eight-person business was purchased by Facebook for $1B, and although the .com has since been acquired, it all started as instagr.am, using the .am domain extension (the country code for Armenia). So there's scope to get creative, but it's worth noting that .coms generally perform better in Google.com search queries. Whatever you choose, you need to carefully consider how your clients will find you.

Username availability across social media platforms

Using social media websites is a useful and inexpensive way to promote your brand and engage with prospective clients, so it makes sense to check the availability of your short-listed names on the most popular websites (Facebook and Twitter being the obvious two). You can quickly check availability of usernames across more than 100 social websites using namechk.com.

In chapter 11, there's a great story about how London-based studio Mat Dolphin used social media and £20 to reach an audience of 374,000 people. It's a useful lesson in how to make these tools work for you.

The legalities

Are there any registered trademarks that conflict with your proposed name? Research your country's intellectual property database and also international databases. Here are a few links: www.uspto.gov, www.ipo.gov.uk, and www.ipaustralia. gov.au. If you're going to use your personal name, this isn't such an issue. It's your name, after all: You don't need to trademark it. But it might be a problem if your name is David Airey and you want to become an independent graphic designer.

How it sounds

Try the name on for size. Answer the phone with it. Introduce yourself at an imaginary pitch meeting. Test the name on a trusted focus group of peers (not necessarily for an, "Is this 'The One'?" call, but more for, "Can you understand what

I'm saying?" feedback). Can people pronounce it? Does it roll easily off the tongue?

Spelling

The easier it is for people to spell your brand name, the easier it will be for all forms of written or typed communication. My surname's not the easiest, and I'm forever spelling out A- I- R- E- Y on the phone, but it's short, and that helps.

You want a name that is also easily searchable. If your new brand is Rendezvous, for instance, you are going to lose a lot of potential customers simply because they don't know how to spell your name.

Memorability

Google, Virgin, Pepsi—concise, distinctive names that are easy to remember. What about in the design profession? Pentagram, Chase, Landor. Notice how these names say absolutely nothing immediate about the product or service each company offers? The more generic names (like New Dawn Graphics) are too obvious, too cheap. There's nothing remarkable about calling yourself Logo World. You want your brand name to help you stand out, not blend in. Look to the companies you want to emulate, and learn lessons from those you don't.

Meaning

Does the name make an emotional connection with your audience or evoke a particular reaction? Have you also checked for cross-cultural meanings or urban diction- ary definitions? The last thing you want is to be known as another unfortunately named brand, like SARS, the drink made by Golden Circle that shares its name with severe acute respiratory syndrome, or SEGA, the computer console that translates as *wanker* in Italian. It depends on your market, of course, but ramifications can easily go beyond your own personal dilemma: Remember that your name does become tied with that of clients. I recall when London's Arsenal FC (who had their shirts sponsored by SEGA at the time) were playing a football match in Italy. For the trip they had to change the sponsor's name to "Dreamcast" (a specific console produced by SEGA), for obvious reasons.

Feeling

How does the name make you feel? What are your instincts telling you? Looking back, when I chose New Dawn Graphics, I was thinking about the many thought-provoking dawns I'd witnessed on my Asian travels prior to setting up shop. But that emotional connection was just too personal, and I certainly couldn't explain it to every new client. Instead, I was giving off a hippy vibe, not exactly ideal when I'm expecting corporate clients to be signing checks for thousands of pounds.

Positioning

Think about your brand beyond where it is today. There was absolutely no need for me to include "graphics" in my earlier name. Wolff Olins, Chermayeff & Geismar, venturethree, SomeOne—none of these leading firms tack "design" or "graphics" onto their names. They don't need to. Neither do you. Consider future growth and the services you many want to offer down the line and avoid pigeonholing your business.

Also, think of the employees you might add to your team someday. Would they prefer to work for a company called Sonya Henderson, for example, or one called Moving Brands?

A few final thoughts...

Before we move on to the next chapter, where we look at designing your personal brand identity, I'll leave you with these final words from my friend Bernadette.

> "Names are not simply designed to identify, they really can take us in one direction or another. And so it goes with brand names, book titles, and product names, too. Companies know that names can make or break, that they build mystery, can form the basis of a movement or create cult status. That's why *Purple Cow* is a more compelling title than *Marketing for Today*, and why Innocent was a genius way to begin the story of a juice and smoothie company.

> "A great name can take you places a good name can't. A truly great brand name makes room for a new story in people's hearts and minds and can position a good product beyond its utility.

> "So don't just set out to name your company, set out to name the vision of what you want to see in the world."

Chapter 8

DESIGNING YOUR BRAND IDENTITY

Your brand is you. It's how others see you. And it's a lot more than a simple logo or wordmark (although those are the things that most readily spring to mind).

Your brand identity is the language you use, the smile in your voice when you answer the phone, the voicemail message you record, how you talk about other businesses and people, the sign on your door, the company car you drive, the way you dress, the copy on your website, your website's ease of use, and it's the promises you make (and keep, because when you tell a client you'll do something, you need to do everything you can to deliver).

Your complete identity also includes graphical factors, such as how your website looks, from the amount of white space and the logo at the top to the fonts and font sizes used for the headings and body text. It's how your site functions, too, whether it's simple and obvious to navigate or whether you're showing off your skills with mouseovers and hover effects. It's the grids you use in your invoices and letterheads, and how these relate to every other visual element of your professional appearance. We'll talk more about the myriad other potential pieces of your identity later in this chapter.

But let's start with what many consider to be the hub of a graphical brand identity: your logo.

Your graphic identity

You might ask why you even need your own logo or word-mark. Won't your portfolio do the real talking?

A graphic that sums up in a very basic way who you are is important. It begins to tell your story, and it serves as a very important first impression, long before your portfolio arrives.

Even a very simple wordmark can represent you, your talents, and your values in a meaningful way.

I leave the concepting and design to you. (You'll find plenty of more specific instruction in my book *Logo Design Love*.) But I do want to share some pointers on the process that I learned while creating my own visual identity.

Treat yourself like a client

Just because you're the beneficiary of the design this time doesn't mean the project should run any differently than it would if you were designing for an outside client. In fact, you won't achieve the result you want unless you follow very similar steps. Like any brand identity project, it all begins by asking the right questions, except this time you're the one providing the answers, too. (See the design-brief questions in chapter 15 for specifics on what to ask yourself.)

Aim for the same timeless outcome you're selling to other businesses, because in today's supersaturated visual environment, it's crucial that your identity becomes and stays fixed in the minds of your potential clients. Just because you have immediate access to your own design skills all of the time does not mean you should recreate your identity whenever the mood strikes.

Set yourself a time frame for project completion. When I was in employment, thinking about becoming independent, I spent around a year sketching various design ideas. That's far too long. If I did that with every client, I'd soon go out of business. Give yourself a deadline and stick to it.

Exhaust your options. Don't settle for the first good idea you come up with. Give yourself a proverbial headache by creating at least three or four worthy contenders. And not just sketches, either. Flesh them out. Apply them to communications relevant to your business: your website, your business cards, your invoices, your studio plaque, and so on.

Ask for critiques

When I say you're designing for yourself, in reality, your brand identity's ultimate audience should be those who will interact with your business—your future clients and the creative specialists with whom you want to collaborate. These are the people you should ask to critique your visual identity. These are the people with whom you absolutely must make a good first impression and build a lasting relationship. You might think you've created the best design since Lindon Leader's FedEx logo, but this isn't a work of art for your eyes only. It must strike others in the heart and brain as well. Ask them what they think.

You've got to do it properly, though. I get tons of emails from budding designers wanting me to critique their logos, and that's all I get, too: a logo, in isolation. No description, no context, just a logo. Sometimes I'll receive a few variations in order to choose my favorite, but the general idea across each will be exactly the same, except with a minor edit of some sort.

Those sorts of requests are just asking me to micromanage their project. Do I like sample A or sample B better? I don't know. I simply don't have enough information.

Remember that you are not asking people for their aesthetic favorite. You're asking for an overall, informed opinion on whether the visual identity is appropriate for identifying your business, your goals, and your future success. Show them your designs in context, and offer a description about what you want it to say about yourself.

Don't show an idea that you don't believe works. The worst outcome would be to feel forced into living with a design you aren't 99 percent comfortable with (designers are never 100 percent comfortable).

Think carefully about who is giving you the feedback, because many people do consider design to be the same as art, that is, a subjective work that isn't created to serve a purpose. Those people won't be able to give you an informed opinion. So if you're showing the work online, where anyone can comment, be vigilant in filtering out opinions that are off-topic and shouldn't sway your thought process. The best way to avoid remarks with little value is to choose exactly who to ask, either by sending a personal email or by meeting face-to-face.

But when the criticism is valid, take it to heart. Don't ignore it because it hurts your feelings or shoots down your favorite design or even sends you back to square one. Back in my student days, I used to hate having my designs critiqued. My work was bad, so the feedback was never 100 percent positive. But that's one of the major benefits of a formal design education: You learn to take critical comments on the chin, and that's excellent preparation for the world of client feedback. Almost all feedback is a gift. Accept it gracefully.

Sleep on it

It's almost a cliché: Sleep on it. But it's a directive with a lot of value. Walking away from a design for a day, two days, or even a week will give your brain time to clear its visual palate. You will be able to come back to your designs with fresh eyes and perspective.

Sometimes literally putting some sleep between you and a final decision can make an enormous difference. The life-changing "Aha!" moment of Otto Loewi, a German neuroscientist, came to him in a dream. He was working on the notion of chemical transmission of nerve impulses and had been experimenting on frogs, but the results were poor. Loewi became anxious and unable to sleep soundly.

One night Otto awoke with a picture of exactly what he should be doing. He scribbled a few notes, then went back to sleep. But when he woke up in the morning, he found that his handwriting was illegible. Many working hours passed with Otto becoming more and more desperate to recover his vision. Exhausted, he finally went to bed again.

In the early hours of that morning, the same vision appeared, and rather than make more notes, Otto went straight to the lab to perform the new experiment. His discovery earned him the Nobel Prize in 1936.

Katherine Ramsland, PhD, author of *SNAP: Seizing Your Aha! Moments* (Prometheus Books, 2012), commented about the prizewinner's story:

> "Many creative thinkers have discovered the same thing. The solution arrives—aha!—seemingly from nowhere. Although they seem random, any of us can harness our mental resources to produce them.

> "What shoves such insights from the tip-of-the-tongue to the top-of-the-mind is the mash-up of certain stimuli. For example, you're doing a crossword puzzle. You stall. But at some point prior to this, you had read an article or walked through a store that contained the correct answer. You'd packed stuff into your brain during unrelated activities that can now converge with a puzzle, and bang! You have the answer.

"So, first, do your research. Be diverse. Gather lots of different types of data. Immerse in your field of expertise, but also read something new to you. This 'idea stew' forms your information base.

"Then, before going to sleep, focus on your impasse so you've positioned it in your brain as a puzzle that you want to solve. Relaxing your thinking brain during sleep allows the association areas to reshape the data into new patterns. When you least expect it, an idea will pop. It might even wake you up. I've experienced this 'aha!' even a few days later."

The moral of the story? If you become stuck when trying to generate a design that will identify your business for years to come, rather than working harder and becoming more and more anxious, take a nap or a walk instead. Work on a different project. Read a book. To get the most out of your brain, you need to give it a little breathing room.

Other parts of your identity

The visual identity is just one part of your brand, so don't rely on it to do the job that *you* need to do. This is only the beginning.

In addition to the factors mentioned at the start of this chapter, there is a wide range of other brand touch points that you must pay attention to, including (but not limited to):

- Social media
- Signage
- Emails

- Voicemails
- Letterheads
- Business cards
- Services
- Speeches
- Presentations
- Blogs
- Sales promotion
- Websites
- Trade shows
- Direct mail
- Vehicles
- Publications
- Proposals

Your brand identity is what ties all the visible touch points together in an appropriate, cohesive format. Each piece is a promise you are making to clients: This is me. This is what I represent. If you don't keep that promise or perform ethically, you're scuppered.

On promise-keeping

Chapter 13 shares more on ethics, but the following sad tale illustrates the vital connection between visual identity and promise-keeping. By 2009, Neil Stansfield and his organic British food brand called Swaddles recorded annual sales of between £500K and £2.5M during a five-year period. The Swaddles identity, put forth in packaging, advertising, and other standard marketing media, used the word "organic" and suggested the same through color schemes, graphics, and photos.

But there was a significant flaw with the brand's promise.

His staff of 12 were purchasing pork pies, smoked salmon, and various other food items from the likes of supermarket chains Tesco and Aldi, stripping the boxes and wrapping, then putting the contents straight into their Swaddles Organic branded packaging.

In September 2009, Stansfield was jailed for more than two years. His wife and business partner were handed sentences of community service for the parts they played.

Ultimately, a brand is a promise. And to succeed, you need to keep that promise.

Chapter 9

WORKING FROM HOME VERSUS RENTING SPACE

One of the first things on your mind when you become independent will be where you're going to set up shop. There are two main options, either working from home or renting a space elsewhere, and choosing one is a decision that should be made before you go independent. It must be well-thought out and researched, because each option has its pros and cons.

Working from home

This is how I started in 2005, living in a two bedroom Edinburgh apartment with a friend. My workspace comprised a desk, chair, computer, printer, and bookcase in the corner of my bedroom.

Looking back, I'm sure the space had a bearing on how I handled my working relationships. My clients might not have seen my bed beside me, or felt the fairly uncomfortable wooden chair I was sitting on, but I certainly could, and it gave my clients a psychological advantage when it came to negotiating on price or squeezing me for some additional (unpaid) work.

I knew my situation. It wasn't anywhere near as professional as I wanted it to be. I needed my clients more than they needed me, and I'm sure my clients could sense it. How? With the submissive language I was using. For instance, I'd be far too quick to present idea after idea without asking for compensation, and this despite the fact I knew my work was appropriate.

On some of those early projects my clients would want the opposite of what I presented, but only after showing my ideas to their "other halves" (who would typically have no involvement with the client's business or indeed have any experience of design). So although my clients couldn't see I was working from my bedroom, my less-than-professional surroundings were affecting my ability to have the necessary confidence in the skills I was selling.

There was another downside: I worked where I slept. I talked a little about this in chapter 4, where I mentioned that when you work from home it's difficult to leave your work "at the office." There's always that temptation to check your inbox or put another idea on paper. When you're working in your bedroom, it's literally impossible to leave your work behind.

But working from my bedroom wasn't all bad. In fact, had I not started where and when I did, I wouldn't have progressed to where I am today without having to secure a bank loan in order to finance an outside space. My overhead was incredibly low, and my small savings of a few thousand pounds were enough to see me through any lean spells until my client base grew.

Seven years (and a number of property moves) later, you can still find me working from the comfort of my home, albeit now with a dedicated room in which to do business, closed off from the rest of the house. You might wonder why I've not progressed to renting my own studio space, and I do contemplate it from time to time, but the main reason is that working from home hasn't adversely affected my success. So for me it wouldn't necessarily be "progression," but rather an unnecessary expense that I'd need to factor into project quotes.

A few words of advice when you're working from home:

- Set yourself a time to start and finish, and stick to it. For example, no checking emails after 8 p.m. (this will also help you sleep better).

- Use your lunch break to walk to the nearest shop or even just around the block. It's unhealthy to spend too long indoors, and the fresh air can help you through creative blocks.

- Allocate a space for your office (preferably a room) rather than working from wherever you might be—the kitchen table or front porch, for example. This helps give you a sense of focus when you step into your studio/ office area, where you know you need to get down to business.

- If other people are in your home during working hours, close the door. There are already enough home-based distractions without family adding to the mix.

- If you share your home with a number of others, it'll make sense to have a dedicated business phone number. You might consider a second phone line or cell phone to be too expensive, and if so, with just one phone line installed your service provider might offer the option to have two different numbers, with a different ring-tone for each so you know if the incoming call is business or personal. Another option is to rent a dedicated telephone number for calls over the Internet, where you hookup a VOIP phone to your broadband router or a headset to your computer. You might run into latency-related audio problems, though, so do your research on the best option for you.

- You may need a specialist insurance policy when working from home. As you won't be storing any large amounts of money or stock onsite, it's unlikely to significantly affect your annual home-insurance premium, that is, unless you plan to invite clients to your place of work—then you'll need liability insurance in case anything should happen to them while they're on your premises. Talk to your insurers or a few different ones to compare prices.

- When you're meeting clients, I recommend visiting their place of work. This helps your clients to focus on the project, because the surroundings are already familiar—there aren't any distractions that arise from being in a new environment (new pictures on the walls, new furniture, new views from the windows, and so on)—the focus is the work. It'll also save you money on liability insurance, and such savings can ultimately be passed on to your clients in your project quotes.

- Don't try to hide the fact that you work from home. There's nothing to be ashamed of.

- You might be in temporary accommodations or thinking about moving in the near future. If so, it might be more suitable to use a PO box for incoming mail, rather than the address of your house or apartment. If you're using your own address, don't print too many letterheads or business cards, because they'll be out-of-date after you move.

- Be careful about what music you listen to. Different genres can affect your mood in different ways. I do some of my strongest work with nothing but the noise of the birds outside.

Renting studio space

Securing outside space will mean additional cost for you, but it can actually bring in more revenue. As mentioned earlier, having a real office space, that clients can visit, puts you in a more professional frame of mind (plus you are always motivated by the fact that you have rent to pay). Renting space can actually lead to a steadier flow of clients, because you are out in the business world where others can actually see you.

California-based Meredith Gossland decided to rent an office after becoming too distracted working from home. She is now the only graphic designer in a building with 125 offices. All the other tenants are small businesses, and she has worked with at least 60 percent of them, designing everything from simple business cards to booklets to product packaging. Office rental including utilities costs Meredith $500 per month, but her income increased substantially after the move. The location is a healthy four-block walk from her home.

In addition, because Meredith works in a building with so many offices, there's a roughly 20 percent annual turnover of occupants as small businesses become larger and need to move on. So there's not only a constant stream of potential new clients close by, but Meredith continues to work with those who leave for new pastures.

You do need to be careful about taking on extra rental expense, though. When designer Luke Mysse decided to upgrade his workspace, he signed a lease agreement for premises that had three private offices, a reception area, and a conference room—and he was solo at the time with big dreams but no real plans on how he'd expand. Luke had two big clients, but when one left, and with his combined home and office monthly rental fees totaling $3,700, it almost ruined his business. Luke was lucky, because although he'd signed a lease for a three-year period, his landlord agreed to release him from the contract once another business agreed to rent the premises.

Luke learned important lessons from the experience:

- Don't make business decisions based on ego.

- Don't move into a space bigger than you need.

- If you rent space to grow, make sure you have a plan on how that growth will happen.

- Don't sign a contract for any longer than you can afford.

Now Luke rents studio space that's smaller, cheaper, and closer to home, plus he's opened it up as a co-working spot, with one full-time and three part-time people who rent desks from him. Luke's workspace rent is $100 a month after he collects from the co-workers.

What a difference.

Another example of renting a studio space comes from Tom Actman and Phil Cook—two London-based designers who started Mat Dolphin in 2009. Though their business was a startup, they felt that perception was everything, and they didn't want to appear as if they were operating out of a bedroom. The duo felt they needed to be in the same room to do business properly: to share ideas, talk about projects, argue rights and wrongs, and to develop.

Upon hearing news of their venture, the owner of a printing company they'd worked with for years made an offer they couldn't refuse—free space and Internet in his warehouse, with the trade-off that Tom and Phil would push all their print work to him and help out on the odd creative project.

The premises were a little out of town and on an industrial estate, but the duo wanted a dedicated workspace before they could really get behind the idea of calling themselves a design studio. For eight months they worked out of a lock-up warehouse, with a meat-curing factory on one side and a manure-making company on the other. It wasn't ideal, recalls Tom.

"It was cold, constantly stank, you wouldn't bring a client within miles of the place, and you couldn't leave food anywhere because of the mice—we even came in one day to find a dead one on Phil's desk!

"But looking back, neither Phil nor I would change a single thing if we were to do it again. It taught us to be grateful for what we had. It taught us to be frugal with our money. And it taught us how you can make a little last a *long* way.

"Without that amazing offer, Mat Dolphin might not be here today."

It just goes to show that you don't always need money to pay for rent. If you take time to look around your local area, you could find similar businesses/peers with whom you can trade services in exchange for a space to call your studio.

But the costs associated with property rental don't just lie in the rental contract. You need to factor in extra insurance, parking for clients, the additional phone line, your office furniture, the time and money spent on your commute—and you'll be eating out a lot more, too.

Fit to work

"Take rest; a field that has rested gives a bountiful crop."

— Ovid

Wherever you're based, it's important you look after your health, and I've compiled a little advice from the Chartered Society of Physiotherapy on proper office health.

Every hour or so, do a few exercises to reduce the risk of developing computer-related aches and pains. This will also increase circulation, send more oxygen to the brain, and help you stay alert.

The exercises don't need to be particularly energetic (leave those for when you're not working). I'm talking about simple exercises like shoulder shrugs, chin tucks, standing up and stretching to each side.

You'll spend plenty of hours in your chair, so invest in a good one. Adjust the angle of the backrest so it's inclined slightly backward, allowing you to rest against it comfortably. Don't lean forward.

Ensure that your lower back is supported. If your chair doesn't have a lumbar support you could try making one by rolling up a small towel.

Don't sit for too long. Stand up and stretch every 20 minutes or so.

Your eyes should be level with the top of your computer display, and the display should be straight in front of you if possible.

In addition to following those tips, be sure to drink plenty of water. I'm in the habit of keeping a continually refilled pint of water on my desk, because even the slightest dehydration affects your concentration. Drink a few pints each day.

And visit an optician every two years for an eye test. Any strain on your eyes can quickly lead to tension headaches, and that can quickly lead to nothing getting done.

Chapter 10

LAUNCHING YOUR ONLINE PRESENCE

The days of lugging around your leather portfolio cases have all but disappeared, because your potential clients want to be able to see your work whenever it's convenient for them, not just when you're sitting in front of them thumbing through portfolio pages laid out on a table. You need to showcase your best work wherever there's an Internet connection and allow it to be viewed on anything from iMacs to mobile devices. If it's not viewable, you'll lose the job to someone whose work is.

You need a website.

Your basic launch needs

There are four key elements to every website launch:

- The domain name
- The Web host
- The site design
- The content

Domain

I registered the domain name davidairey.com in 2005, and I renew it every few years. Most domain registrars offer the ability to purchase a name for a period of between one and ten years, sending you an email reminder a month or so before expiration with the option to renew. I also recommend buying your country-specific domain, too, if outside the United States (where .com is generally the norm instead of .us). For instance, I also own davidairey.co.uk—used mainly as a backup (part of my Plan B) as well as to prevent the possibility of another designer named David Airey from competing for local search-engine rankings. Expect to pay roughly $10 to $15 per registration.

Web host

To let others view your Web pages, you need to publish your website. That's where the Web host comes in. You pay your host an annual fee, then upload your files to the company's servers, where they're stored and accessed by online visitors. The fee mainly depends on the amount of traffic you expect to receive. Start with a smaller plan that allows you to upgrade. You can always switch Web hosts if you find the service inadequate, and if you decide to, many hosts offer to move your files at no extra cost, saving a lot of hassle.

Once you have both your hosting account and your domain name, you simply access your domain name settings and associate the domain with the Web host server details your Web host gives you. This joins your domain with your pages. Although there's a wide range of prices out there, expect to pay $150 per year for your hosting.

Many companies offer domain registration as well as Web hosting, but I recommend that you use two different suppliers (one for your domain and a different one for hosting). This minimizes your risk: If something should happen to either company, you have a little more control. Ask other designers where they buy their domains and hosting, because some companies charge a lot more than you need to pay, and others make promises they can't keep.

Design

The design of your website plays a huge role in getting people to view your pages. You want to keep the focus on the information (the words of your story and the images of your work) rather than whistles and bells that more often than not just irritate visitors. If you don't know how to code the design yourself, learn, even if it's just enough to differentiate a template from everyone else who uses the same one.

Here's some basic advice:

- Put the focus on what you're selling. For visitors to turn into clients, they need to know what you can do for them, so add a short intro in a high-visibility area.

- Use dark text on a light/white background. It's easier to read than white text on a dark/black background.

- Avoid trying to control typography by setting text within images. If your potential clients have poor eyesight they won't be able to scale the text to a comfortable size without the text becoming pixelated, and search engines won't be able to read the words you display (unhelpful for searchability).

- Don't fall into the designer trap of using tiny text sizes. It's not easy to read, and if a visitor can't read what you're offering, you won't get hired.

- Show some cohesiveness between your website design and the rest of your brand identity. For instance, if the logo on your website is in the top left corner, put it at the top left of your business card and letterhead. Use the same typefaces, similar margins, and so on. It's all a part of brand consistency.

- If you show third-party advertising (one of the additional income sources we'll look at in chapter 20), keep it low-key. There's nothing worse than arriving at a website filled with animated banners and unexpected pop-ups. Have respect for your self-image.

Content

At a minimum, your site needs to contain the following:

- Homepage: Your homepage is a visitor's connection to every other part of your website. It's also where those who don't know you or what you do start to gain an understanding.

- About: This is where visitors get the key facts they need to interact with your business. It's where you write like you talk, because it's *you* that's on show—not some robot accompanied by a stock photo of two people shaking hands. Include at least one photo of you, and if you're brave (with solid video skills), embed a short video introduction. The use of video can quickly build trust with people you're unlikely to meet face-to-face.

- Portfolio: Show only your best work. I've seen too many portfolios cram in so much mediocre work that the best projects are overlooked. I recommend including around ten solid projects along with an explanation of why your work helped the client to win new business. Keep images to a high quality and size, but when saving, optimize them for Web viewing so your pages load quickly.

- Contact: A zoomable map helps people see exactly where you're based. If working from home, you might choose to keep your address off your contact page, keeping it hidden until after initial client discussions. That's fine, but be aware that the more open you are, the more trust people will have in your professionalism.

These are the four essentials. No independent designer's website is complete without them.

Two more pages I recommend adding include: testimonials and a blog.

The best advertising: word of mouth

Testimonials build trust and can be a powerful force when clients are deciding between you and another designer. Clients want to know who else you've worked with and what your working relationships have been like. They want to know that their hard-earned money is in safe hands, and that once they pay the initial deposit, you won't ride off into the sunset.

Of course, it's possible for anyone to fabricate such third-party comments, and some unethical people do, thinking that the more comments that are on show, the more people will believe their product or service is worth buying. But fakes are easy to spot, and there are few faster ways to turn off a potential customer.

I do two things to help improve testimonial credibility:

- I provide a link to the client's website.
- I show a photo of the actual person I dealt with (when available).

These are two small details, but they can make a big difference.

Perhaps you don't yet have a large enough selection of testimonials to create a separate page on your website, and if that's the case, you can always display what comments you do have alongside the respective projects in your portfolio.

The incredible value of a blog

Inclusion of a blog is something I recommend to any designer, particularly as my blogs are why you're reading this book (my publisher contacted me in 2009 after visiting my Logo Design Love website, which led to the creation of my first book, and now, a second one).

There are a variety of blog platforms from which to choose, each with a huge number of online tutorials that will help you set up your own. WordPress is the platform I've been using since the launch of my first blog in 2006, but you might prefer Movable Type, ExpressionEngine, or Typepad; there are many others. Do some research before choosing the best fit. I've stuck with WordPress because it's easy to get the hang of and it does everything I need.

England-based designer Chris Spooner started his first blog a few months after I started mine. He's been successfully self-employed on the back of what is now a small collection of blogs, and he's an ideal case study for backing up why I think these online tools can be hugely beneficial.

Chris told me that since its creation in early 2007, his blog has always been his greatest source of clients. "I used it as a place to post design tutorials, to experiment with design, and to share the tips and techniques I've learned along the way. It's easy to assume that posting free tutorials that explain how to do something that you're otherwise charging for in your freelance work devalues your service, but in fact I found it was quite the opposite."

There are three main ways Chris's tutorial posts directly benefit his work as an independent designer. First of all, the tutorials gain good exposure in the design community because people share content they find interesting or valuable with their friends, so creating posts that explain sought-after design techniques naturally spread across Twitter, various social bookmarking websites, and other design blogs. This increases backlinks and traffic, which helped rocket Chris's domain up the search-engine rankings, resulting in his design portfolio gaining more exposure to potential clients browsing on Google.

But it's worth remembering that clients finding you through Google can generally be of a lower quality than those who seek you out specifically.

"Clients via Google were often just looking for 'someone' to build their website—they were rarely interested in my design expertise and essentially wanted me to be their puppet. I realized my best clients were those who valued my design knowledge and who had chosen me for my design style. This is where my blog really helped. All those tutorials that were being shared across the Web were drumming up exposure for me as a designer. People were beginning to recognize me and relate my name to my particular style of work."

Clients were now contacting Chris because they specifically wanted him to work on their projects, and it was easier to delight them with the results because they already knew what to expect.

"Prospective clients weren't looking at my portfolio anymore—they were getting in touch after reading my design tutorials. It soon reached a stage where I could post a tutorial on a particular topic, then receive a handful of project requests based on that topic. For instance, a logo design tutorial would cause a collection of logo design projects to appear in my inbox a few days later."

A specific example is when Chris published a tutorial on creating a skateboard deck design. It was a format he had no prior experience with, and was just something he fancied trying. A man from a company who produced merchandise for the band Fall Out Boy saw the tutorial, liked Chris's work, and got in touch to ask if he'd be interested in creating designs for a skateboard deck, a T-shirt, and a hoodie for the band's new album launch.

"This kind of project was something I never would've landed without the exposure my blog had generated."

Hard-won lessons

Looking back, it's easy to spot the mistakes I made regarding my website. Follow these simple tips, and you'll fare better.

#1 Publish a blog

I know I've already spoken about this at length, but it's that important. I launched my first website in 2005 under the guise of New Dawn Graphics (mentioned in chapter 7). The site had around 15 to 20 static pages with info about the services I offered, a showcase of past design work, and some relevant contact info.

That was it.

Nothing more.

No way to generate discussion or build an audience, and that's precisely where a blog excels. Without one, I wouldn't still be in self-employment.

#2 Use a self-hosted blog

For three months in 2006, I made use of the freely available blog service at WordPress.com, pointing people from my then static website at davidairey.com to the frequently updated posts I was publishing at davidairey.wordpress.com. But my blog was held by WordPress; that is, it was on the WordPress servers along with some limitations as to what I could do with it (regarding the design, the plug-ins, the flexibility for new features).

When I realized the limitations, I ditched the WordPress-hosted blog and downloaded the freely available backend files from WordPress.org. I then uploaded the files to my own Web hosting account where I had unlimited access and control over what changes could be made.

#3 Don't assume people will visit

I had no idea how to gain new readers and commentators. I had the impression that if I published new content, I'd automatically attract readers.

Wrong.

First, I had to devote a lot of time reading and commentating on related blogs. For my own blog posts, I had to search for information that others would find interesting, then put my own spin on it. That's a key point—adding your own thoughts. Anyone can regurgitate the same content that's found elsewhere (many do), but only you have your thoughts. Use them. Share them. It's why people will return to your website— because of you.

You'll soon discover there's a whole psychology behind blog publishing, and it changed my way of thinking. Nowadays, if I see or hear something of interest, I wonder how I might incorporate it onto my blog.

#4 Write like you talk

My first blog on WordPress.com included articles that were more like lectures. Who wants to read a one-way lecture? That won't get readers involved in a discussion. I want to learn from what my readers have to say, and hopefully impart some useful information in return. In the beginning, I was killing the conversation instead of making use of my blog's comment threads.

I still regularly visit a host of other blogs and join the chat. It takes time, but people appreciate comments, and it helps build relationships.

The way you write, the words you use, your tone of voice, how you respond to comments, the design of your blog, the topics you cover…they all show who *you* are. Be open. Be friendly. Be the person you want others to know you as.

#5 Stay put

You'll need to decide the location at which to install your blog. I first installed mine at davidairey.com/blog, in a directory titled "blog." Your Web host should offer you the ability to create new directories, naming them whatever you like—"journal," "news," "articles," or whatever.

Think of directories like shelves in a bookcase: You can arrange things on those shelves in whatever manner makes the most sense.

My problem arose when I discovered that most of my incoming traffic was to the blog. It made sense to move the blog's location to my root folder, davidairey.com. That meant I had to move my portfolio off its original "shelf." I created a directory titled "portfolio," because to me it was a better idea to place the most popular element of the website—my blog—up front and on the homepage, and then let people move when they wanted to go to davidairey.com/portfolio to see my work.

That was all fine and good from an organizational standpoint, but there was a definite sacrifice for me in terms of search engine recognition. Here's why:

Google assigns a level of trust to websites and their individual directories: The more hits, the more trust, and the more your directories/shelves move up in the world of search recognition. When I moved the blog location, I was losing a lot of what people refer to as "Google juice," because the original blog directory was now defunct. The new blog location had to start building Google trust again from square one. In effect, I was starting from scratch with regard to search engines, and this was after about one year's worth of post publishing.

The lesson there is to be as sure as possible about where you want specific installations to occur, whether they are in the root, in a directory, or even in a subdomain, such as blog.davidairey.com. If it's a dedicated directory or subdomain, be sure to allocate a name you're unlikely to regret. For example, you might not want to use "notes" because your blog may develop into more than just a "notepad."

#6 Don't underestimate the time commitment

I had no idea how much time authoring a blog would take. I jumped right in without doing any research, and it's a simple reminder of my naiveté when I revisit my old and uninspiring WordPress.com blog.

Now I spend approximately ten hours per week managing my three blogs at davidairey.com, logodesignlove.com, and identitydesigned.com. That might seem like a lot of time for publishing one or two new posts on each website each week, but that's only one part of the game. In addition, comments need to be moderated (approved, edited, or deleted), and I do all I can to reply to as many as possible. I'm never 100 percent satisfied with the design and layout of each blog, so I tinker (you'll find this difficult to resist). And I often revisit old blog posts to bring them up-to-date (fixing broken links or changing a few sentences).

Treat your competitors as allies

"It is amazing what you can accomplish if you do not care who gets the credit."

— Harry S. Truman,
33rd President of the United States

I love sharing the work of others on my websites. Some people have asked if it hinders my ability to attract new business, believing that potential clients will hire those I'm promoting instead of me. I look at it like this: My clients are smart. If they think another designer or studio is a better fit for their needs, then they're probably right. Besides, there's a lot of business for all of us.

Sharing work I admire not only helps motivate me to improve my own design, but it continues to build my blog readership because it turns my website into a source of inspiration for others, too.

In addition, people like free promotion, so when that's what I give, I go a little way toward building a relationship with those I feature—a relationship that can prove beneficial if I'm approached by a potential client who wants something I don't have the skills to deliver.

You can never do everything your client needs. Remember that.

Your client will need to work with other people, and if you can offer a recommendation, it benefits everyone involved: You're considered knowledgeable and a good partner, your clients save time they would've needed to spend researching, and the person you recommend earns more money.

You still need to vet potential clients before sending them to someone else, so keep the red flags from chapter 14 in mind. I've unwittingly sent red herrings to several designer friends for which I later had to apologize.

At the same time, you need to take care before vouching for a designer, because your reputation lies in their hands (if they do a bad job, it ultimately reflects upon you).

Chapter 11

MARKETING YOURSELF AND FINDING GOOD CLIENTS

One of my biggest worries in business is where the next client will come from. It was a worry when I started, and it's a worry seven years later (albeit to a much lesser degree).

When one approach doesn't work, you need to learn from it and move on to the next idea. For instance, my cold calling door-to-door with nothing but a stack of flyers and a positive attitude was woeful. It soon became obvious it wasn't working. So I stopped.

One approach that did work, however, was to scan through local newspapers and trade magazines, looking for the adverts with the worst design (there were plenty, and you'll probably find the same). I'd cut out the ad and send it to the company who placed it along with a mockup of how I could make their ad look more appealing within the same space confines, coupled with a few sentences about hiring me or buying the artwork's copyright. In many instances, all it took was a follow-up call to get a foot in the door and earn some cash. It led to the start of some local business relationships, too, and they can be vital for generating word-of-mouth referrals.

Marketing yourself is about demonstrating that you have the talent, skills, qualifications, and experience to make a real difference to your potential client's business. Thankfully, there's a huge array of approaches you can employ when trying to clinch your next deal. In this chapter, I share smart ideas from experienced design business owners.

Go pro bono

Many designers in employment are bound by their contracts so they can't show designs they did for their employers in personal portfolios. It's a standard condition in employment contracts; the employer retains full rights to the work.

So I'm often asked how designers in this situation can build a portfolio. After all, how do you attract clients if you can't show them your work?

That's where pro bono design plays an important role.

What is it?

Pro bono publico (usually shortened to pro bono) is a Latin phrase meaning "for the public good." The term is generally used to describe professional work undertaken voluntarily and without payment as a public service.

Unlike traditional volunteerism, pro bono uses the specific skills of professionals to provide services to those who are unable to afford them.

I recommend offering your skills to local nonprofits, because international organizations will have a dedicated budget for their design work and are much more likely to hire a designer or studio with a comprehensive portfolio.

When Connecticut-based Gary Holmes started out, he made a conscious decision to work with local companies at first. He offered to do some pro bono work for Noah Webster House, a local history museum. The museum team liked his work and was soon hiring him to do paid design jobs. And as the museum was highly visible in the local community, the exposure quickly led to other client referrals for Gary.

Oakland-based Lita Mikrut was starting her freelance career when her daughter joined a youth golf program run by a national nonprofit with local chapters. Lita could tell it had substantial potential to reach children and teach core values.

Lita was receiving the program's announcements via email, usually Word documents sent as attachments. A two-page document arrived one day, and curiously, the second page was completely blank. She could see an opportunity and contacted the program's executive director, offering her services pro bono.

"This was one way I could give back to this program, which was in its infancy locally, and truly needed support," she recalls.

Over the course of a year, Lita created a few thousand dollars worth of pro bono work, creating a set of branded collateral that could be repurposed with each new fundraising effort.

"The executive director was moving across the country, so I introduced myself to the new director, and continued my role as their designer. The role became a paying gig, I think because of my sincere dedication and the fact that our collective efforts did increase their funding, and has, in part, kept the program alive."

In addition, the original executive director ended up taking the same role for a chapter in her new city, and she brought Lita on board as the chapter's designer.

So, what started out as pro bono work to help her daughter's after-school group ended up becoming two paying clients who are doing great educational work with youth.

Although Gary and Lita ended up with paying clients, it's important to remember that pro bono design is for the greater good, and that a sense of "doing good" in your community (with no ultimate financial reward) is a feeling that is hard to top.

For two years running, London-based designer Jenny Theolin set aside four months of her extracurricular time to devote to the Design Business Association's Inclusive Design Challenge, when she would work with care centers and nursing homes to develop a new generation of inclusive products, services, environments, and communications. Here she explains why:

> "Described as the 'combined Oscars and Olympics of the inclusive design world,' this is not to be confused with a normal design industry award. The Challenge didn't offer me any promise of an end product beyond the satisfaction of taking part and designing 'for the greater good,' 'for our future selves,' and of being at 'the cutting edge of innovation.'

> "The Clinic London trio I was part of won the 2010 Challenge, and our work was featured in the resulting exhibition in London's V&A museum and has since traveled all around the world.

> "However, we made absolutely no money. Nor did we win any new business as a direct result. In fact, as an agency we lost both money and agency time (quite ironic considering the Design *Business* Association had organized it).

> "From a business perspective, it made no financial sense to take part. But not only did the Challenge inspire the individuals on the team, it also fired up the rest of the agency I was working with—we were doing a project that *really* meant something.

"So why dedicate your time to getting involved in an unpaid challenge such as this? Well, I can without a doubt say, and hopefully I speak on behalf of the others who took part, that it got us out of our habitual design processes, and ultimately made us better and happier designers and creators. We rose to the occasion, stretched ourselves, and through hard work satisfied this burning desire to create something *we* were happy with."

Pro bono design doesn't get those important bills paid, obviously, so let's look at some marketing efforts that led directly to designer income.

Love the ones you're with

Karishma Kasabia of Australia-based Kish+Co understands that marketing today needs to be savvier than traditional marketing methods, especially when it comes to keeping relationships with existing clients flourishing.

"No one wants a shitty flyer or an average postcard. We need more to catch our attention, and even more still to be loyal and to love a brand.

"The best and often most unloved place to start is with existing clients. We're used to their attention; we're much more sugar coated when we meet the potential new ones. That's not right.

"For Valentine's Day, we had custom cupcakes made for our studio, then mapped out our existing clients, from the outer suburbs of Melbourne and all the way back into the core of the central business district.

"One hundred cupcakes, with orange and brown icing based on our corporate colors, individually boxed with a Kish+Co seal were delivered. We started at 9 a.m. and finished at 6 p.m., hand delivering to suppliers as well as clients. I drove and double-parked; my partner Agnes did the delivery.

"That same day we got Tweeted and Facebooked, and received calls for new work, recovering our marketing costs for the day's effort with one single job.

"The best thing is how memorable we made our brand."

You'll discover that owning a small business makes you very stringent when it comes to expenses. But as Karishma recommends, you need to measure the results of your marketing, whether it's tracking hits with a pricey placement in a marketing magazine or a creative treat costing you about $500. It can often be the cheaper, more creative endeavors that bring the best results.

Market for free online

Mark Bloom of London-based Mash Creative spent more than 12 years working for other people before deciding he wanted to be his own boss. The problem, Mark said, was finding the work, but he didn't let that deter him.

"When I complete a new project I will often approach design blogs with a view to getting it featured. I will also upload it to my Behance account. Showing off your latest work allows potential clients and other designers to see that you are constantly trying to push the boundaries or better yourself from your last piece.

"Ever since setting up Mash I have firmly believed in the power of social media and design blogs. Around 25 percent of my clientele is based in the United States, most of whom approached me after seeing my work on the Behance network or on a design blog. I have been fortunate enough to have several of my projects featured on the front page of Behance over the years. This exposure takes your work outside of the country you're in, showcasing it to a worldwide audience.

"Black Watch Global, an American intelligence and risk management consultancy, approached me to rebrand its existing identity after seeing one of my featured projects on Behance. The rebrand was quite extensive, consisting of identity, stationery, and a 40-page brand-guideline book. I wouldn't have got the commission had my work not been added to Behance."

Mark and I have both found the incredible value of sharing your projects online, as nowadays (and for the past four or five years), the vast majority of my clients find me through my online presence.

A little research, a lot of return

Antoinette Marie Johnson of Philadelphia-based At Media made a list of all the companies she knew that were just starting out or that needed great improvement to its brand messaging. She researched each entry on her list, and with that information in hand, her team designed its marketing collateral and Web sales materials to speak directly to those on the list. Then Antoinette set out on a mission to reach them both in person and online. Since then (2009), At Media has continued with that strategy, resulting in an average annual growth rate of 84 percent for the small agency.

Here are some of Antoinette's tips on how to compile your own list.

1. Subscribe to local business journals, blogs, and so on. These publications are sources of relevant industry news regarding businesses in the area. They sometimes also provide a yearly "Book of Lists" that details the most successful businesses to know in the area, their decision makers, and industry and recent new businesses.

As an example of how this pays off, At Media attended a "40 Under 40" business event that highlighted local executives under the age of 40. One was the CEO of CheapCaribbean.com. Despite the dot-com's incredible success and a valuation of over $500 million, At Media knew it could still use an agency's help (it had poor Web design, little advertising, and no mobile app), so Antoinette personally mailed the CEO a congratulatory letter. One week later, she was sitting at a meeting with the co-founders, and her team was enlisted to start branding the new client's newest project.

2. Scope out any businesses in your immediate area that look like they need your help. Even if they seem difficult to track down, you're likely able to help them in whatever expertise you can find. Look for a mutual friend who might work there or already be a vendor.

Antoinette compiled a list of the top five businesses in her immediate area that could use At Media's help. She went to several events these businesses might be attending and just mingled as a regular networker. She handed her card to the vice president of one of the businesses, and two months later received a call to discuss graphic design and a new Web presence. The firm has been an At Media client for more than three years now and has since grown tremendously.

3. Know potential clients' needs and don't push them into things they don't need/want. Know what these companies are doing, and what their brand message is, as well as their key focus and income. Find out if they're launching any new divisions or areas of growth. It's important that you demonstrate that you've done your homework. Just like at an interview for a job, you must show that you know why you came through the door (rather than just showing up to make the sale). Listen carefully; you might not land the deal you were expecting now, but there could be excellent opportunities later.

4. Identify the decision makers. The "about" page on the company's website is the first place to look for any leadership in a company. Sometimes you'll even get lucky and find direct contact information. Don't hesitate to use it. LinkedIn adds new business-to-business search features every day. Use them. Search for the company, any connections, and most important, any mutual connections you might share. Maintain good online etiquette: Don't connect with someone just because they are connected to another person you know and then privately message the unknown party to make an introduction. Just seek out the connections through existing connections, and you'll be surprised how fast referrals will come.

It's who you know

Stellan Johansson of Sweden-based 1910 Design & Communication shared how he struck up a relationship with his first clients.

"During our last two years of in-house work prior to becoming self-employed, we saw a trend of game developers needing services like ours, almost to the point of companies competing over the relatively small number of user interface (UI) designers with AAA game development experience available.

"Our initial business plan centered on using our established network of people to offer services like identity design and UI design for games and creative developers as a starting point for our business.

"Of the 12 projects we've completed during our first 6 months, 10 have sprung from connections, recommendations from former co-workers, and the kind words of friends."

Similarly, most of the first projects I worked on after going it alone were the result of people I knew from my time in employment or through friends and family—a website for my uncle who owned a pub, and a range of posters for a music event organized by a friend of an old boss, to name just two.

Make use of your address book. Tell people you know that you're in business for yourself. It can really help get you started.

Reach out to other design agencies

Steven Key of England-based Key Creative was previously employed in a studio for many years. During those years, he found there were always peak times in the year where work was liable to get outsourced in order to make deadlines, such as when coworkers were out on holiday leave.

"When I first made the jump to self-employment, I figured that this could well be the case for a lot of design companies. So I made lists of localish agencies and printers and sent them letters, a business card, a little contact form, and a self-addressed stamped envelope. I would send these out a week or two before the peak holiday periods, and would always get a much higher success rate when compared with mailing out at other times of the year. The timing is key as it sows a seed in people's minds. And, when the rush jobs hit and people are on holiday, it seemed to trigger the memory for the possible solution—that is, the letter I sent.

"I still receive requests for work from literally the first set of these I ever sent out over six years ago."

Zig when others zag

Others might be marketing with postcards or flyers or websites. Wouldn't it make sense to head off in a completely fresh direction?

England-based designer Andrew Kelsall is another professional who targeted design agencies. He made a list of a few he'd like to work with on a freelancing basis and spammed them. Literally. He mailed Spam by putting the agencies' addresses on the cans of meat along with a stamp. That was it. Nothing else. He repeated the process after a few days until the companies he targeted ultimately received about five cans each.

The next stage of Andrew's marketing plan was to mail a Spam-branded folder showing a photo of a can of Spam bearing the words, "You've been spammed." Inside was a copy of his résumé and a cover letter that explained who he was and what his design skills included.

Andrew was invited to work on a freelance basis with Leeds-based Wobble Design, and when he turned up on the first day, he was told it was his Spam marketing that got him the contract.

Offer a real gift

Cincinnati-based Adam Ladd has been a professional designer since 2003, and in 2011, he took up self-employment. At that time, he had barely any exposure or online presence. His passion was creating brand identities, so to play to his strengths and promote his business he produced a short video that he could share with potential clients. It showed a variety of well-known company symbols. As each was displayed, he asked his five-year-old daughter Faith for her opinions of the symbols. Faith's commentary proved to be a delight in a video titled "Fresh Impressions on Brandmarks (from my five-year-old)."

After Ladd uploaded it to YouTube and shared the link with a few design blog authors, it proved a huge hit. It attracted more than 1,000,000 views in one week and became a "trending" video. Soon, it was featured on websites for *Adweek*, Brand New, Huffington Post, *Time*, Wolff Olins, LinkedIn, PSFK, *Business Insider*, Jezebel, Shutterstock, *Branding Magazine*, swissmiss, and many more.

Adam increased his Twitter followers from 80 to 1,080 in just one week, and he received multiple Q&A requests from a variety of blogs. He even landed a video interview on the TV show *Right This Minute*. And, of course, quote requests for his services came in from around the world.

Think fast

When Tom Actman and Phil Cook started Mat Dolphin they made the conscious decision not to use a single piece of design work created while working for their previous employers. Tom recalled, "Awkwardly, we had no website and no work to show people, let alone much to talk about. We knew that in order to get recognized, we needed great work, or a great client list. Those can take time to nurture, though. So in the meantime, we realized we needed to exploit other avenues to raise our profile."

That's when the duo made use of Twitter and social media. Using social media and writing a blog are two quick ways to help establish your voice and opinion. They slowly but surely started interviewing people in their "Ten Questions" series on the blog and were sharing content from other designers and studios on Twitter. Bit by bit, they were connecting with the people they respected.

In February 2010, Tom was stuck at home suffering from the flu. While checking the Mat Dolphin Twitter feed, he noticed that *Creative Review (CR)* had tweeted celebrating its first year on the social media platform. It gave him an idea.

"At the time they were one of only a handful of magazines exploring social media, and they were sitting pretty on some 50,000 followers. That's a lot of people listening and reading content away from their website. I called Phil and told him we needed to design, print, and drop round a poster congratulating the magazine on its achievement. We knew the publication was based around the corner from our studio, so it seemed like a nice way to say well done and possibly a way of letting them know who Mat Dolphin is. Phil designed the poster in record time and ran around the corner to get the poster printed while I tweeted them that we had a celebratory surprise coming. In less than two hours from seeing their tweet, we'd designed, printed and delivered a poster to their door. Thirty minutes later, they'd replied to us on Twitter and sent around a photo of the poster on the wall of the *CR* office. Not quite instant fame, but we'd made some friends and they thanked us by email. The poster cost us £20 and a little bit of creative time."

Mat Dolphin kept in contact with the *CR* team and let them know when they had any news to share. Things got interesting in May 2010 with the launch of a new Mat Dolphin website. The designers told *CR* about it, and the staff tweeted the launch to what was now a *CR* Twitter following of almost 100,000. The traffic they drove that day not only crashed the new site, but every other one that was also on the shared server. By the end of that day, Mat Dolphin had some 5,000 hits and suddenly people knew they existed. The design firm's own Twitter following increased as a result, and people were reading their blog and liking their work.

"Since then, our relationship with *Creative Review* has blossomed. In May 2011, once again via Twitter, they ran a competition to guest edit their Twitter account for one day. Leap at the chance? Of course we did. After getting through the first round of questions, we were narrowed down to the final against three others. We eventually won, and on Thursday, May 26, we were in charge of the *Creative Review* Twitter feed, reaching some 374,000 followers.

"It didn't stop there. Suddenly Mat Dolphin became a name people knew. In July 2011, we were invited to take part in *CR*'s Blast/Bless Tate Britain exhibition and have since been invited to numerous other show and events. In addition, *Design Week* shares the same publisher and office space as *Creative Review*, so we've been able to make friends there and have been featured on the *Design Week* website, offering opinions and feedback on design-related news."

All of this for spotting an opportunity, making the most of it, and investing just £20 to get a poster printed.

Do business where you shop

Independent designer Suzana Shash has been freelancing for two years. She kept a lookout for businesses in her neighborhood that were starting up, or who didn't have websites or compelling brochures or menus.

Her first client was a salon in a trendy area—one that had no website but was always offering group buying coupons. Suzana made an appointment to get her hair done and talked to the owner about it while he was working on her. She ended up getting hired to create a website and a business card design. Since that first client, a lot of Suzana's website traffic has come in from the salon website, as she still has her "designed by" tag in the footer, and she has received design requests from other spa owners in the city who followed the link from the salon site.

When things go wrong...

Karishma Kasabia of Kish+Co shared another marketing experience, but this one didn't give the intended results. It took place in August 2011, when the studio changed its business name from Miss Kish to Kish+Co. She planned a launch party that would include an artists' exhibition, some food and drink, and hopefully, lots of new clients in attendance.

Long story short, too many artists (and their friends and family) were in attendance, enjoying the spread, and far too few clients showed up. In fact, AUD $30K (USD $29K) later, exactly no new clients were secured.

Looking back, Karishma reflected, "Sometimes, I feel our existing clients have really breathed life into Kish+Co, and we hadn't really celebrated them. I would love to lavish our profit on them and on our team. Those are the people who really deserve it. Now, I'm careful to measure up the numbers and be honest with myself about outcomes prior to embarking on any marketing exercise. It was a hard lesson to learn, but it's been the best thing that has happened to me since I started the business. I can now call myself a savvier business woman."

Lee Newham of London-based Designed by Good People is another who learned from a marketing plan gone wrong. He thought it would be a fantastic idea to go to trade shows in an attempt to win business from the exhibitors. The problem was, everyone he approached was too busy selling their own services to potential clients. That plan was quickly abandoned.

Even when things don't go according to plan, you can still learn valuable lessons.

Chapter 12

WHY BIGGER BUSINESS ISN'T ALWAYS BETTER

Back in 2005, I wanted to portray myself as a design agency, one with a full staff who could cater to a multitude of client needs. My website copy was written in the third person, too, so as to imply that I was more than me.

What an idiot.

Sure, I planned to build and call upon a network of designers on an "as needed" basis, and that was my rationalization for posing. But to put it bluntly, I was basically lying about who I was and how I worked.

My business was me. No one else. For some reason, I thought that if I showed myself as working alone it would hinder my ability to attract new business. In hindsight, I should have embraced being in a company of one, because there are many benefits to being small.

From the outset, I made the mistake of looking to the wrong role models for me. I wanted to grow to a size the likes of a Pentagram and a Landor. There's nothing wrong with that, and if it's what you want, brilliant. Go for it and good luck, but be certain that this is an accurate reflection of where you truly want to go. Ultimately, such growth didn't coincide with my true desires. I just didn't know it at the time.

It took me a year to realize my goal was to grow *me*, not to expand my company in terms of numbers of other people. As such, more appropriate role models for me were the likes of Lance Wyman and Milton Glaser, designers known by name for the work they create, the commentary they offer, and the inspiration they give to designers everywhere. In his book, *Speak Human* (smashLAB, 2009), Eric Karjaluoto remarked, "We mimic the behavior of those who have achieved a position we too would like to reach. The challenge with this is

that we confuse the affectations with the cause. Although a wealthy person might have a Bentley, it's unlikely the car made them rich. Similarly, a big company may have really nice offices, but it's a mistake to think they are successful because of those offices... Is there anything more ridiculous seeming than meeting someone from a three-person company who introduces himself as the CEO?"

In short, be honest. Be who you are: a talented designer with plenty to offer. There are specific advantages to running a small/one-person office, advantages that are very attractive to clients.

The personal touch

Tokyo-based Richard Knobbs made the same mistake I did when he went independent as K Creative, portraying his business as larger than it actually was. But he soon reaped the rewards when he put himself at the forefront: All of his clients appreciated the more personal, familiar touch.

The stronger the relationship you can form with your clients, the easier it becomes to win new business. You'll find your working days will become more enjoyable, too. So when you're true to yourself, you'll attract the clients who know *you*—not your imaginary or someday or even real staff—are the right person for the job. As such, there'll be much less difficulty in reaching a successful project outcome. Person to person, you will work it out.

In addition, when clients call, text, or email, they get you, not some junior staffer or secretary who can't help them. There's real value in that.

You are what clients want

Think about it. The most experienced people in many large design agencies are spending their time out clinching new business, not creating design. When work is won, it's often passed to less-experienced designers in the company, because the people who win the contracts are out gunning for more.

But when *you* win a contract, it's *you* who plays the key role in every stage, from concept to completion. Use this as a selling point because clients appreciate knowing that you'll be with them each step of the way. It's a very streamlined and efficient way of working, and clients recognize that.

London-based designer Lee Newham notes, "The head of design at supermarket giant Tesco, who is now head of design at a large drinks company, told me Tesco wanted to talk to companies whatever the size, that small was good, different was good, and that small companies that tried to be like the bigger agencies annoyed them. They wanted to talk to the smaller guys *precisely* because they were small—to get a different perspective."

Running with the big dogs

Throughout my time as a sole trader, it's become obvious that you don't need to be part of a big business to work with large organizations. Those large organizations just don't care what size office you have: If the work is solid, they will hire you.

In 2008, I received an email out of the blue from a senior manager at Yellow Pages Group. With online revenues of $346 million and 2,700 employees, it's a huge business. After some emails back and forth and a few phone calls, the company became my largest client at the time, and I worked on refining the well-known "walking fingers" logo.

In 2011, again through an unexpected email, an external relations specialist at the Asian Development Bank (ADB) got in touch. With $21.72 billion in approved financing in 2011, and more than 2,900 employees from 59 countries, this was another mammoth enterprise. Some emails and conference calls later, I started reworking the brand identity for ADB's Annual Meeting.

So just because you work independently, with a simple website as your main marketing tool, you don't need to limit the size of the firms you want to work with. But rather than wait to receive such work inquiries, be proactive: Approach the businesses you want to design for. You have nothing to lose.

Quality control

As businesses become larger, it's more difficult to tell who's pulling their weight and who's hiding behind others. Eric Karjaluoto wrote in *Speak Human*, "Toss in some memos, meetings, and office politics, and it gets harder to determine whether a staff member is kicking ass or just great at kissing it."

But in a company of one, there are no coworkers to shield poor performance.

Your only choice is to be outstanding. You are completely in charge of quality control.

Forget big—be solid

You want to make it clear that despite your small size, you still have the capabilities to surpass expectations. Publishing client testimonials and in-depth portfolio case studies helps. But what if you don't have a great number of these to use?

On my website's "about" page I mention that I've appeared in design publications such as *Creative Review*, *Computer Arts*, *HOW* magazine, and a few others. This helps build credibility with potential clients. You can do the same. Approach trade magazines and offer to write a special feature on the niche you've chosen. Magazines will often pay their writers for contributions, but even if you don't receive monetary reward, it's a valuable form of promotion that helps to align your name with your skills, and to an audience you wouldn't have otherwise reached.

Other simple ways to prove your solidity:

- Be early to meetings.
- When preparing a quote, a presentation, design artwork, or any other deliverable, tell your client when to expect receipt, and don't be late.
- If a client wants two corporate color options, offer a third.

The clients you deserve don't care about size. They want the best person for the job. Make sure that person is you.

Small means agile and passionate

Big firms don't have the agility you do. It's possible that after a few years of running your business that you find you've become more passionate about a different design niche. Due to your size, you can start targeting your desired client base immediately. Now imagine if a large brand consultancy wanted to do the same. There'd be meetings, negotiations, potential layoffs and new starts.

Huge payrolls require a continuous focus on finding new work, so it becomes much more difficult to twist and turn in line with the passions of the business owner. You, on the other hand, don't have the same outgoings. You can put all your effort into just a few brilliant clients, creating fantastic work while making a healthy profit. And because you're taking on less work, your clients receive more of your time and attention, helping the process run more smoothly, resulting in clients who love what you do.

In large companies, the passion gets diluted, because it's rare when an entire team of employees has the same passion for the brand as the person who launched it. When you're the only person responsible for delighting your clients, the passion is as pure as it gets, and your clients will reap the rewards.

Remember that once you start adding employees and growing the number of people in your business, it won't be so easy returning to a company of one if you discover that's what you prefer.

Chapter 13

LEGALITIES, INTEGRITY, AND MORALITY

The design profession can be a bit of a jungle when it comes to ethical considerations. There's no governing body to lay down a set of rules or guidelines that we're required to follow. No professional accreditation is needed before we can call ourselves designers.

Other professions, such as architecture, law, or medicine, require those who practice to pass exams, but it seems fashionable for anyone to call him- or herself a designer, regardless of their day job. "I designed a flyer for my church," "I designed the layout for my living room," "I designed some T-shirts for my new clothing line," and more can be heard from people who've no idea about kerning or CMYK.

Just because I can fix a leaky faucet doesn't mean I get to call myself a plumber.

Don't get me wrong. Everyone has a capacity to design, the opportunity to learn and become exceptional. But the wide difference in numbers between those who actually do strive to learn more and those who think formal education isn't necessary means there's a common misconception among lesser clients that anyone with a computer can design. The good part is the people we choose to work with aren't those lesser clients. We (should) only work with those who understand the value in our profession and who know the importance of hiring the right designer (you). (It's easy to spot clients you don't want to work with, and we'll identify those red flags in the next chapter.)

Regardless of the lack of predefined "rules," we owe it to ourselves, to our clients, and to the success of our business to understand the critical issues of ethics in graphic design.

Legalities

Legal issues can be complex, and they are changing all of the time, but you do need to pay close attention to them.

In her book, *Ethics: A Graphic Designer's Field Guide* (self-published, 2010), New York-based designer and teacher Eileen MacAvery Kane cites traditional copyright laws, which grant exclusive rights of ownership for 50 years, offering protection to copyright owners. She also notes that Larry Lessig, copyright lawyer and chair of Creative Commons (a nonprofit corporation offering ways to grant copyright permissions for creative work that make it easier for people to share or build upon the work of others) has challenged these laws, contending that they're antiquated and out of sync with contemporary culture. Lessig and other Creative Commons advocates feel that current copyright law actually creates a culture of lawbreakers with a complete disregard for the law and the consequences that might ensue.

How might this apply to you and your business? Take your blog as an example. Of course, in a visual business, it's important to use images to generate interest. For years, rightly or wrongly, I published images belonging to others without first asking the creators for permission. I did so because one of the things I like to do is share design work I find inspiring and worth discussion. Granted, I always made sure to give credit to the owner in the form of a byline and a link to his/her website, but I was publishing without permission, and according to those laws that Lessig deems antiquated, I was doing so illegally.

Was I punished for my actions? Throughout the years, only once was I asked to remove an image (the aggressively protected Formula 1 logo, even though I was highlighting it as good design). It's much more likely that when someone sees his or her photo or illustration published on another website that they are happy for the promotion and link. This can be considered "fair use" under the Copyright Act of 1976, but distinction between fair use and infringement is not easy to define.

Generally, the safest course of action is to always get permission from the copyright owner before using copyrighted material.

Another instance where legalities play an important role is in font licensing. When so many fonts are available for free, a lot of clients believe it's okay for designers to readily send them any font file, including those created by professional typographers and font foundries. In order to legally supply a file to your clients, you must have a multi-user license and explain to your client the installation restrictions—that is, the file can't be installed on a limitless number of computers. It's your job to either dissolve the cost of the multi-user license into your overall project fee or to explain the restrictions to your clients, pointing them toward the website where they can purchase a license themselves.

In addition, stay vigilant when a printer asks you to send a font file, because unless you have a license for multiple computers, or unless the font license allows for printer distribution, it's illegal to email that file, just as it's illegal to share a piece of computer software.

Keep in mind that just because a font can be freely downloaded, it doesn't mean you can automatically use it in your client projects. Free fonts have licenses, too, and they might contain a restriction that states they can only be used for personal or educational projects (i.e., not in for-profit work), so be sure to read the accompanying license in order to avoid paying damages. Contact the vendor if you have questions.

Then there's plagiarism in graphic design, the unauthorized use or close imitation of existing artwork and the representation of the artwork as one's own original creation. Eileen MacAvery Kane relates one of the most well-known cases, when artist Shepard Fairey used a photograph of Barack Obama and stylized it for a range of posters. The photograph belonged to the Associated Press (AP), who wanted compensation from Fairey. But he sued for a declaratory judgment that the poster was fair use of the photograph. The two parties settled out of court in 2011, before in 2012 Fairey pleaded guilty to destroying and fabricating documents during the legal proceedings.

American Institute of Graphic Arts (AIGA) medalist Ellen Lupton recalls when she was asked to be an expert witness in the case by the lawyer representing the Associated Press.

"This was a case of artist vs. artist, and I could really see both sides of the story. On the one hand, shouldn't any picture of Obama be considered part of the culture, fair game? On the other hand, didn't the photographer work hard to get that particular shot? I said no to the request. Too much moral ambiguity. Later, it came out that Fairey had lied about which picture he used. The morals become far less ambiguous, and Fairey ended up embarrassing the free-culture side of the argument. Not cool."

When your blog gains a decent level of exposure online, you're sure to come across unscrupulous idiots who scrape your blog's content in its entirety, republishing it on their own websites, where they've added some Google AdSense (an ad-serving application where the publisher earns money per click) or another form of advertising in the hope of earning a few dollars from your hard work. In my own case, there are so many sites doing this with my content that it would take longer to chase them all down than it would to continue with doing my own work and creating more blog content. I put it down as "one of those things." If you prefer to go after the fools, more power to you.

Integrity

Designers have a number of integrity-based decisions to make on a daily basis on topics such as doing spec work, digitally altering images, negotiating client contracts, and coming to terms with what our responsibilities are to our clients and colleagues.

Avoid spec work

Integrity is about adhering to your principles, and one of my main principles is to steer clear of spec work: work done for free, in the hope of receiving payment (volunteer work or pro bono design, as discussed in chapter 11, is a different matter). I think that because graphic design is a profession we love, many people with a need for our services think designers will happily work for free. I often receive emails asking for just that. Free work. Here's an example of one such request:

> "We've partnered with a top English DJ and producer to offer graphic designers the opportunity to participate in a worldwide project for which they can receive global recognition for their creativity.

"The project asks that graphic designers design the official logo for [the DJ] that he will use on all of his merchandise and marketing material worldwide during 2011. The selected designer will also receive $1,000 (USD) for their design."

It prompted me to reply with a unique opportunity of my own hoping to highlight the inanity of the situation:

"Thanks for the kind offer.

"In return, I'm reaching back to let you know about a unique project opportunity for [the DJ].

"The project asks that [DJ] record and produce a new music track—one that mentions my name and my title as a graphic designer. I'll play the track on my website to a worldwide audience, giving full credit. I'll also pay $1,000.

"If I don't like the track, or if I prefer one created by another DJ (I'm contacting thousands of others with the same unique opportunity), I won't play it on my site. Nor will I pay the monetary prize.

"To participate, have [DJ] send the completed MP3 file to my email address."

Imagining how spec work plays out in another profession often makes it seem like a very foolish request, and unsurprisingly, I never did get that MP3 (but do I keep receiving similar requests from other people).

Get it in writing

It's imperative that client expectations are met throughout the course of a project. The most effective way to ensure this is by having a written agreement for every project. This agreement should describe the scope of the project, the time frame, and the costs. We'll detail the terms and conditions you need to highlight in chapter 17.

Sometimes fulfilling the agreement can be painful. JP Jones of Oklahoma-based Paige1Media recalls when her then-newly formed business was working with its first official client. JP and her business partner were still learning the ropes of small business leadership and feeling their way through contracts and proposals. The client requested a quote on a bilingual design project, the pricing was accepted, and the two part-ners arrived on site to discuss the job. It didn't take them long to realize that a huge mistake had been made. Through poor communication, the duo had misunderstood the client's request and quoted the project on a set of totally different parameters.

> "My business partner looked at me and I nodded my head slightly. He went on to offer to not only match the price we had quoted but to take full responsibility for the misunderstanding of the project. By taking the ethical high road and a hit on that one project, we not only gained the trust and loyalty of that client, but now, years later, they continue to be one of our strongest clients and have referred more than two dozen other clients to our firm over the years.

> "We often wonder what would have happened if we had handled that project differently and had not risen to the occasion—taking the responsibility for our own learning curve in the client jungle. The money we didn't make on that single project has been paid many times over—there is no price too high for showing that your firm stands behind its word—even when you make mistakes."

Trust your gut

When Liza Lowinger and Spencer Bagley started Brooklyn-based Apartment One, they had a clear vision of working with clients who are "giving back" and "doing good" in big and small ways. "These are broad concepts that can be expressed through many different means," Liza pointed out, "but of utmost importance to us is working with clients who approach their business with integrity."

Years ago, Liza and Spencer were presented with the opportunity to redesign a website for a client specializing in private security training with the goal of enhancing their consumer appeal. At the time, Apartment One was a small, growing agency, and while this client and project didn't align with the duo's vision, the opportunity to work on a large-scale project with a big client was appealing. They also felt pressure to accept the project because an individual interested in purchasing their agency had referred the job.

> "If we didn't agree to the project, we risked alienating ourselves from someone who we saw as a central player in the future growth of our company.

> "Spencer and I grappled with the decision. Our intuition, that inner voice of truth, was leading us to a clear place of no; however, the promise of financial reward and business security at an early point in our business made us question our decision. In the end, Spencer and I agreed to hold firm and remain true to our position. We passed on the opportunity, and as a result ended our relationship with the person who had referred us.

> "A few months after we turned down the project, the client started appearing more frequently in the media and underwent much public scrutiny. The experience

and subsequent outcome reaffirmed to always remain
true to our core values and 'trust our gut.' This was an
important lesson that continues to resonate and that we
share with our clients in our work to support them in
identifying and expressing their truth and uniqueness."

You also have a responsibility to those with whom you collaborate, and to those you recommend to potential clients
that you're unable to help personally. The foundation of all
successful design is solid relationships, whether that's with
your client and his/her team, with the illustrators, photographers, or copywriters you work alongside, or the designers
you choose to pass leads on to (you can quickly burn bridges
if you waste a designer's time with poor referrals).

Morality

London-based designer Miles Newlyn chooses not to work
with zoos or companies involved in warfare. Interaction
designer Guy Moorhouse takes a similar stance against
tobacco or gambling firms. I won't design for politicians with
agendas I don't agree with.

These are all choices based on personal morals, and they're
rarely black and white because we all have our own stand-
points, born from different life experiences.

It can also be difficult to know every last scrap of information about a client. And how much research can you afford
to carry out before deciding to accept a project, because how
long would it take to ensure that each and every client acts in
accordance with our own morals?

One of my earliest clients in self-employment was an online
company that compiled links to downloadable eBooks.

I think my naiveté showed in accepting the project, because after publicizing my design online, I came in for criticism from others who told me that links to their eBooks were offered through my client (links pointing to third-party websites distributing the PDFs for free without author permission). This may have been an isolated mistake made by my client, but if my research had been more thorough prior to accepting the job, would I have made a different decision? What if I had found out about the problem halfway through the project?

Italian illustrator and designer Andrea Austoni told me how a particular publishing house asked him to design the logo for its Bible Study iPhone app, and another wanted him to design the logo of its Children's Bible comics app. Andrea is strongly against organized religion, especially its teaching to children, so he politely told both companies that he had to decline their offers.

These kinds of questions aren't easy to answer sometimes. We all have bills to pay and families to support, so it can be a very personal decision about where we draw the line in our own interpretation of right and wrong.

If a newspaper firm or a book publisher approaches you with work, do you question your potential client on the toxicity of inks or the origins of the paper used before accepting the project? What about if IKEA gets in touch? In her book, Eileen MacAvery Kane commented on the furniture the company sells: "The unsubstantial wooden slabs and wobbly table tops are a marketing ploy—the furniture is not supposed to last—and consumers are comfortable with this. The argument that IKEA's popularity is due to answering consumers' needs is a shortsighted one. IKEA is not the answer; it's a fix... The unsubstantial products age [when trends change] and break and the need for replacements emerge." From a prestige standpoint, you might consider yourself a fool not to add IKEA to your portfolio when given the opportunity, but then again...

California-based designer and teacher Robyn Waxman says it well:

"My biggest ethical issue concerns whether I am brave enough or care enough to follow that trail of manufacturing to learn that the product or service I am about to promote is the very thing that undermines me and what I care about."

Section III

HOW DO YOU MANAGE PROJECTS?

Now it's time to get up close and personal with your closest business allies (and occasional enemies)—your clients.

All the prep work you've done will count for nothing if you can't handle the client presentation, the terms and conditions of a contract, the schedule, client expectations, delivery of the finished goods, the collection of payment, and more.

Chapter 14

CHOOSE CLIENTS WISELY

It does cost money to turn down a project, but saying "yes" to the wrong client can be equally as costly. We have only so many hours we can devote to our profession, and working with the wrong people means you don't have time for more enjoyable and potentially more profitable jobs.

As the late motivational writer Stephen R. Covey, author of *The 7 Habits of Highly Effective People* (Free Press, 2004), once said, "Doing more things faster is no substitute for doing the right things."

A case in point, to illustrate why saying "no" can be the right move. A prospective client approached a studio in London called ico Design with a new food retail concept (he'd seen some of the studio's work for other food clients and was interested in working with the team). The prospect had recently sold his flat and had a substantial amount of cash to back his idea. In the initial client/designer meeting he talked through his concept, his ambition, the people he saw as potential customers, and even where he might open his first store.

"From the outset, alarm bells started ringing, especially given that something like 90 percent of all new food ventures in London fail in the first year," explained ico's Russell Holmes.

"His concept was incredibly niche, yet he imagined that it would be something that would appeal to everyone. His business model demanded something that no food outlet could ever guarantee: that customers would visit every single day. When we questioned him about the likelihood of this, he got extremely defensive. His food was going to be great, healthy, and tasty. Why wouldn't everyone want to go every day?

"We took stock internally. This man obviously had ambition and wanted to work with us; however, we felt that if he went ahead with his idea, it would almost certainly fail. Design was

a critical part of his concept, so if it did fail he would surely look to us as bearing some of the responsibility."

Rather than take the man's money and get involved with a potential white elephant, ico Design decided to approach him with a proposition. In a follow-up meeting, the ico team expressed its doubts about the retail concept. They suggested that the client pay ten percent of ico's proposed fee. ico would conduct some research and suggest if and how the concept could be improved. He agreed, and as ico predicted, their research showed that the public was not the slightest bit interested in his proposition. ico turned down the job.

Financially, ico did not profit as it might have, plus the team had no new work for the studio's portfolio. But the decision was the best course of action in the long term. Sometimes it's better to step away from a project that is potentially flawed than to get involved purely for money.

But Holmes notes that there is still a potential upside. "We took a gamble that this particular client would look favorably on our good advice should he ever want to start up another business."

Red flags

Here's an excerpt from an email I received earlier this year:

"Do you have a money-back guarantee? Because I've already worked with two companies but I'm not satisfied."

I've fielded thousands of inquiries, and a statement like that is a definite warning sign of a potentially difficult client. It hints that I, too, might be asked for a refund after the project started. Also, because this person was already unhappy with the work of two other companies, how likely is it that he would be happy with my design? Of course, there's a chance that the other work was not good, but there's also the chance that the problem lay with an impossible-to-please client. There are other sorts of clients to avoid, and when necessary, fire.

Mr. Too-Good-to-Be-True

Northern Ireland-based Darragh Neely has been running his own design practice since 1997. He recalls some telltale signs of potential nightmare clients.

"The promise of large—and too-good-to-be-true—amounts of work further down the line in return for a small piece and usually free or very cheap design; indications that the client has been 'round the houses' already and has visited a number of your contemporaries to no avail; outrageous claims of success; name-dropping; and the intimation of limitless funding for your work. Finally, it is likely that your ego will have been scratched to within an inch of its life: Phrases like, 'I've heard great things about you,' or, 'You come highly recommended,' are commonly misused in conjunction with any or all of the above."

In one particular example, Darragh took a call from a potential client early in 2012. Let's call him Fred. Fred was itching to meet the design team. He sounded rather eccentric, a little excitable, and was at pains to point out that his "exciting" project was "very urgent." Intrigued, Darragh obliged him with a face-to-face appointment a few days later.

"Fred looked and behaved exactly as I thought he would after our brief phone conversation. To begin with, he spent a good few minutes gushing about our work, making special note of the fact that we had been recommended to him by a friend. When pushed as to the origin of the referral, he very cleverly sidestepped the answer. It would have been rude to pursue this, and I assumed he would tell me at a later date. Even after 19 years in this business, my BS-ometer only slightly twitched. In hindsight, this was flag number one."

Darragh accepted the brief. It was for a product Fred had been developing for some time, and although it seemed a little unpolished and somewhat "bonkers," Darragh thought it could be raw enough to leave some scope for a nice bit of branding and packaging.

"Fred's enthusiasm and excitement was almost infectious. It made me forget that I had doubted his intentions, albeit fleetingly."

Fred was given a date by which he could expect to see some concepts, along with an estimate of costs to which he immediately agreed. Work commenced in the studio in the normal way, and the ideas began to flow. The designers started to research the product competition, inspirations and Fred himself. Flag number two began waving, not because of what they found, but because of what they didn't find.

"Some of the outrageous claims our client had made just didn't stack up. Nevertheless, we kept working, caught up in our own excitement and eager to please and reach a solution.

"In the interim, Fred had been in touch. He was pushing—a little too hard for my liking—for visuals early for 'an important meeting.' He had cleverly contacted one of our designers directly rather than me, saying he wanted them emailed, another warning sign. A face-to-face presentation should always be employed for the first reveal. This gives you control and protects your work. It also gives you the ability to control any decisions. Flag number three."

Darragh refused the request, and Fred was told the designs weren't quite ready. The number of flags was increasing, and concerns were voiced within the design team, but they kept working.

"The information that came back over the next few days was startling. Fred had been to at least two other agencies, one of which was uncomfortably close to me. I decided to talk to both agencies directly. It's worth noting that although healthy competition exists in the local design community, we still look out for each other. It transpired that ideas had been generated over an extended period of time and, in both instances, the design house had parted company with Fred with no money having changed hands. By this time we had reached quite an advanced stage in the process: A set of highly polished and 'almost ready' visuals were at third iteration, ready to send for sign-off."

The conclusion Darragh reached was that this guy was milking every designer he could get his hands on for ideas without paying a penny.

"I tackled Fred directly on my findings—not an easy thing to do, believe me—and despite his protestations informed him that we would no longer be continuing with his project, my only solace being that we had not let visual material leave the studio, electronically or otherwise."

If there's a lesson to be learned from Darragh's experience, it's to take heed of any apprehension you have over a particular client. "It's still possible to get it wrong regardless of how much experience you have. Nobody wants to fire a client, but it's easier to do early rather than late, so look out for those flags."

Darragh has had to make the decision three times during the 15 years in which his company has existed. Regardless of how good a designer you are, unless you're incredibly lucky, it's a situation you're unlikely to avoid.

The Jekyll-and-Hyde client

Tim Lapetino of Chicago- and Los Angeles-based Hexanine is another experienced designer who has had to fire a client. Hexanine was engaged to create a new community website centered on women's issues, specifically, issues surrounding the perception of their bodies. "We loved the concept as well as the cleverness and verve of the founder, and how we might be able to really flex our creative muscles. In the early going, we were also very encouraged by the fact that this client seemed to *get* the process. Our client talked the talk, understood the lingo, and seemed very responsive to what we proposed, as well as our process. A love fest, you might have said."

But the tide turned almost immediately. As soon as the designers began putting pencil to paper, the conflicts began. The only part of the process that didn't draw complaints, confusion, mid-course corrections, and yelling from the client was the initial sketch concept round. "The client wasn't happy with initial design rounds, so we redoubled our efforts on many subsequent rounds, and sought to dig deep into unexplored territory, and out of that came some excellent work that will never see the light of day."

For Hexanine, one additional round became ten, a few bonus concepts turned into many, and they agreed to waive their normal practice of curbing scope creep in order to please the client. But they couldn't land on something the client would approve, and the criteria devolved from stated business goals to gut hunches that couldn't be predicted, based on whims of the moment and ethereal catchphrases.

"After quite a lot of work, we settled on an identity concept that was part of one of our ideas, but not wholly, and attempted to make it work. The client was still not happy with the mark, but for the sake of time, we pressed onto the website, naively thinking that it would be a better arena to work in, because we had specifically limited the scope. We were wrong.

"The site was even more of a disaster, and we couldn't wrangle the client to choose specific items and commit to certain styles, and all pretense of goals-based decision-making went out the window. The client was picking what they liked, and what was 'liked' turned out to be terribly ugly. We protested and fought, but in the end, acquiesced."

Hexanine was contractually bound to complete the website, and did so, but the studio will never attach itself to any of the outcomes.

"The work isn't right for the specified audiences, and it ended up being designs that were dictated by one very opinionated client."

The client treated Tim's people badly. There was yelling, terse emails, blaming, and anger when Hexanine didn't respond immediately to weekend emails. There were even accusations of spying via Skype because the client didn't know how to use the software.

Tim later discovered that the team was actually treated much better than most of the client's vendors. Several PR agencies had been fired and suppliers bullied.

"For some reason, maybe our desire to keep things civil, we were spared the worst of it. But of course, we heard later that the client had bad-mouthed our firm to others as well.

"This project might *still* be going on if not for our decision to bow out and end our relationship with the client. We did as much as we could to deliver on the client's brand promises, but the working relationship wasn't producing good results. We tried to exit amicably and with as much grace and care as possible, but the same fate seemingly awaited anyone who worked with this client."

Tim learned these lessons from the experience:

"Be flexible, but don't subvert your own time-worn process, even if a client seems like they will work with you on it. Our process is our safety net, source of strength, and the basis for keeping things on track. We diverge from it at our peril, especially if a client requests that we do so.

"We learned to always do our due diligence with clients. If we had spent some time researching, we might have found some of the negative online comments about this client, allowing us to approach the project with our eyes wide open. Now we make sure the things other people say about prospective clients are things we're comfortable with."

Mr. Wrong

In another example of a project gone wrong, Fiona Burrage of Norwich-based The Click Design Consultants shared a "firing" incident from some years ago when The Click was commissioned to rebrand a firm of estate agents. To give a little background, the studio's usual payment terms were half on commencement and half on completion. The client agreed, but upon asking the team to begin, flatly refused to pay.

"At this point, it may have been best to stick to our principles and walk away. However, this was a prestigious client who promised further work, and we did not have the benefit of experience we now possess."

The Click started work on the project, returning with several options. Finally, one was chosen after a period of negotiation. Shortly after and completely unannounced, the creative director at The Click received a startling and extremely rude email from a partner of the client who had not been involved in the project so far. The 15-point email stopped just short of demanding that the entire project be redone. Fiona remarked, "We were perplexed but told by our original point of contact to ignore it and carry on, albeit with a bitter taste in our mouths."

Next came the second stage of the process, where preparations were made to roll out the rebrand. The Click team found themselves working to incredibly specific instructions provided by a client who was beginning to make design decisions on their behalf.

"When we did what we thought best, it wasn't good enough; when we did what the client asked, it didn't work and we were to blame. After several months of crisis meetings and numerous iterations of a particular two-sided document, we felt at a loss as to how to please the client. If we sent them an email, it would either be returned instantly with a barrage of criticisms or ignored until work was required for the next day. Each part of the project was subject to numerous rounds of amends containing increasingly proscriptive instructions. As a result, studio morale was at an all-time low. We felt our hand had been forced."

At this stage, the team decided enough was enough, and for the good of their business they called a meeting to fire the client. They wanted to remain as professional as possible, agreeing on a mutually acceptable payment and offering to hand over everything that was created so far—InDesign files, notes and guidelines—to enable another agency to continue the work.

"Unfortunately, the client became rude and abusive, replying with words to the effect of, 'You're really starting to f**king piss me off now.' Point proven, we quickly left their offices, settling the final invoice and transferring work at a later date as agreed."

Other nightmares

The descriptions above certainly do not define the entire universe of problem clients. Ireland-based graphic designer Sheena Oosten shared five red flags she watches for.

1. Clients who are extremely slow to respond

Responses with short, monosyllable answers or project briefs that are non-specific or extremely abstract are early signs that the project could become difficult down the line. If a client is unwilling to answer a few simple questions regarding their business and their goals, then they're likely just fishing for the cheapest quote.

2. Clients who micro-manage

Client input is vital, but some clients are merely looking for nothing more than a pixel pusher. The client knows what he wants in his head and is simply searching for a designer to translate an idea into a digital format. A popular response from these type of clients would be, "I'd do it myself if I had the time, but I'm just too busy." These clients can be very difficult to please. Similarly, those clients who tell me how long the project/job should take and what they expect to pay are often clients who don't understand the value of the services I provide or don't respect what I do.

3. Generic emails addressed to multiple others

The client is simply looking for the cheapest quote. If they don't have the decency to address me in their email, or if they call me by someone else's name, or haven't taken the time to view my work, then chances are good they're not particularly interested in working with me.

4. Beware the clients who have fired other designers

It's always best to determine why the last project didn't work out, whether it was down to the client or if it was due to a "cowboy" designer. I always try to see it from both sides before agreeing to take on someone else's project.

5. Clients who constantly question my rates

Those who haggle on price or expect a ridiculous amount of work for the cost of a small lunch are never worth entertaining. Similarly, those who repeatedly question a request for an initial deposit or those who are very slow to pay the deposit can often be difficult to extract final payment from.

It is never easy to walk away from a client, no matter what he or she has done. On one occasion it left me feeling anxious, as if I was doing my client a disservice, when in reality, I'd already done much more than we agreed upon, and had been much more flexible than with any other client. It's important to remember that if you keep bending and bending to suit client demands, something will inevitably break.

With experience, you'll be able to sniff out problem clients, too. Give it time. The unfortunate part is that it will take a few red herrings before you get really good at it.

Chapter 15

HANDLING THE CLIENT APPROACH

If you let it happen, potential clients can waste a lot of your time before you realize it's better to say "no" to their job. But there are ways to filter inquiries that save you and your prospects a great deal of wasted energy, which allows you to focus on clients who are a better fit, and which allows those unsuitable prospects to get on with finding a more appropriate designer.

The client questionnaire

A questionnaire is essential. It should be the first thing on your mind when an approach is made because its completion will give you a detailed understanding of your potential client's specific design needs.

Questions to ask

Here are some items I like to include.

How does your company make a profit, and what is the structure of the business?

Remember, this is an initial questionnaire, and you'll need to ask follow-up questions. The aim of the first question is to give you a rough overview of the company's product(s) and/or service(s). In addition, knowing a little about the business structure can help you to determine how many people will be involved in the decision-making process. For instance, is this a one-person startup or a multinational with a board of directors?

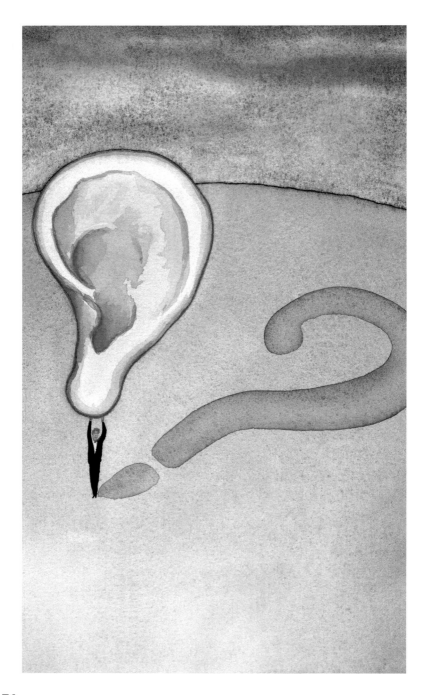

Is this a new design or a redesign of something that already exists?

If it's a new design (be it a new brand identity, a new website, a new annual report, etc.), then you'll have more of a blank slate on which to form your ideas. A redesign or refinement, however, will require that you see the original designs.

What are your goals for the project?

Client expectations and how you surpass them play a huge part in the success of any project. You need to discover exactly what your client hopes to achieve, whether that's a 300 percent increase in new business inquiries during the first year or something less specific, like the launch of a new visual identity that's more appropriate for the future goals of the company. The more specific and measurable the expectations, the better for both parties when it comes to judging success, but there are always more factors involved in the success of a product or service than design alone, so it can often be incredibly difficult to measure the impact you have on a client's business. That said, just because it's difficult doesn't mean you shouldn't try.

Who will be working on this project with you?

The ideal scenario is where you're dealing with the sole decision maker, the person who can give the final approval on your work. It won't always be possible—particularly when dealing with larger companies—but beware of committees where a number of people have equal input, because this can lead to severely diluted designs, replacing the remarkable nature of what you bring to the table with something that just does the job.

We'll look at presenting your work in more detail in chapter 18.

What is your target completion date and why?

Generally, you need to set the time frame. You'll have a better idea how long the project will take to complete, but this question allows you to keep expectations in check.

There might be a trade show on the horizon, or perhaps the launch of a new product. This may mean that your work needs to be completed before those preset dates, and there is no flexibility in the schedule. When the completion date is unrealistic, you need to explain the time involved and how it's important to get the job right rather than rush and make unnecessary mistakes. You're integrating the client into your process, not the other way around. As such, you need to maintain control of how the steps are followed.

Who is your target audience and ideal customer?

You and your client will drive the project forward together, but remember, every choice you make needs to be in consideration of the client's customers. You need to know who will have the most interaction with the website, the visual identity, the mobile app, and so on. Who do you need to research and understand? Whose attention do you need to attract? Does your client intend to reach a new type of customer? Is a current design inappropriate for the intended audience, or does it simply need refining?

Who are your competitors?

This is something you can find out through research on your own, but it helps both parties to get these important questions answered as soon as possible, so let your client share the workload (a design project is a joint venture after all). The work you produce will be more effective when it can be judged in the relevant marketplace, and if your client is to win, there needs to be a loser (the competition).

What are you worried about?

By addressing any concerns at the outset (perhaps they have never worked with a designer before, or there is in-house worry about changing an established design), you can help put minds at ease. With less worry, there's more confidence and a stronger possibility of achieving the best result.

There'll likely be other preliminary questions you want to ask, but don't go overboard. Sure, you need to learn as much as possible, but this is just the first step in what will become an in-depth process. It's the step I take before even talking to a client on the phone or meeting in person.

Delivering the questionnaire

There are a number of ways to deliver your questions.

- Host an online form
- Email a PDF or Word document
- Offer the document for download

You might want to integrate one, two, or all three of these options into your process. In the past, I hosted an online form (and I might do so again in the future), directing clients to that particular page of my website. The advantage was that the formatting of the answers was consistent, and I had the ability to incorporate "required fields" so all questions were addressed before the "send" button would work. An online form also eliminates one step in the process, allowing a client to submit answers before you need to personally send the questions.

The disadvantages with Web forms are that they can go offline if there's a problem with the host provider; they can't always be saved or stored by the potential client; and Internet connections can drop unexpectedly, sometimes in the middle of completing the form. If you had just spent 20 minutes completing a form and the info was lost when you tried to send it, would you bother again? Some online forms are divided into a number of pages, with each page automatically saved before the user moves onto the next one. That's an option.

I prefer to email a Word document. I'm less concerned about the formatting and more concerned with delivering and receiving the answers in a way that suits how I work. That one extra step doesn't concern me, because it's an additional opportunity to rule out potential red flags, and as soon as a Word document is received, it's right on a client's hard drive to be tackled in his or her own time.

I tried using interactive PDFs, where questions were followed by text fields, but there were continuing problems on the prospect side with saving and sending, so I avoid those now.

The completed questionnaire won't tell you everything you need to know about the project (there'll be follow-up questions you need to ask), but it should tell you a lot, and it will also show how serious the prospect is about working with you (half-baked answers are a definite red flag indication).

Avoid wasting time

When your profile is raised and you gain higher search-engine rankings, you will attract an increasing number of inquiries about your services. Unless you can afford a secretary, it's you who needs to read, consider, and reply to each and every email (although with time you'll know which ones to delete right off the bat). Your aim is to find out as soon as possible whether the lead is legitimate, or whether someone's simply looking for a price to justify hiring someone cheaper.

Regardless of the legitimacy, you'll often be asked for a price before anything else is discussed, but of course you won't be able to offer a quote until you know project specifics. In order to cut to the chase without giving the impression you're fishing for the highest profit, there are two ways to determine if the two of you should proceed:

1. Give some indication of what it normally costs for other clients to do business with you. This might take the form of a minimum price (the smallest amount you'll be happy to accept a job for) or a more general price range (from "this amount" to "that"). Be aware that when you do this, you might be shoehorning yourself into a specific box that is difficult to climb out of. Don't undervalue yourself. Web and digital specialists Happy Cog previously showed a minimum project cost of $100K at the top of their client questionnaire. There's no doubt it filtered out a huge amount of unsuitable prospects and saved the firm a ton of time.

2. Ask what budget your client has available. Sometimes this can be answered (such as when a design strategy was previously planned and budgeted). Sometimes it can't, especially when a potential client has absolutely no idea what it costs to hire a designer. Either way, you mustn't be afraid to ask.

Start on the right foot

There's a chance the prospect won't have made the decision to hire you until after the questionnaire stage and after you've talked in person or on the phone, so if you can provide evidence of how you work with clients and what role clients take in your process, it can have a big impact on getting to "yes."

Alina Wheeler, author of *Designing Brand Identity* (Wiley, 2009) and *Brand Atlas* (Wiley, 2011), developed one piece of paper about her process that changed her life and her approach. The page is a kind of flowchart divided into five numbered sections: conducting research, clarifying strategy, designing identity, creating touch points, and managing assets. Each section lists a number of steps/actions to be implemented.

Why did it have such a profound effect? "Because of its simplicity," Alina said. "The process can be daunting if you have never gone through it. And potential clients see themselves in the process, which more than anything, builds trust in the whole team and the fact that a disciplined process with key decision points will be used to achieve results. It also gives clients a map as to where they are in the process, what they can check off, what decisions are needed before you begin the next phase, and so on."

There's one cardinal mistake Alina sees all the time: teams failing to establish clear goals and an endpoint. "Why are we doing this? How will things be different at the end of the engagement? Especially during lengthy engagements, people forget why they are making the investment."

She uses straightforward language to communicate these goals, as demonstrated by the following samples she wanted to share with you.

Staying on course

"We recommend that we have one key contact person throughout the process. It is critical that all decision makers participate in the audit readout and brand brief sessions."

Commitment

"We will work collaboratively with your leadership and business development team to achieve results."

"We will develop a working protocol and schedule that is aligned with the way you like to work."

"We will always seek simplicity, differentiation, and sustainability in our solutions."

You could say the whole client approach and how you deal with it comes down to managing expectations. Our websites present an image of who we are and what we do, so even before we get that initial email or telephone call, the person on the other end has already formed some idea of what he is going to get from us.

If a client expects something that I don't usually deliver, and he or she hasn't specifically asked me for it, the project isn't going to run smoothly. It's up to me to find out exactly what the client expects.

Chapter 16

PRICING YOUR WORK

"How much should I charge?" That's probably the most common question I'm asked. Every few days another email arrives from a designer struggling to price his or her services.

I struggled too, and even today I'm sometimes left doubting my quotes. Did I undersell myself? Did I price myself out of a top project? I'm sure I've done both, lowballing my services until my confidence grew, then slapping a higher-than-usual price tag on what I offer, to the detriment of the deal. It's a balancing act we all need to play, and one that we only learn the rules of through on-the-job experience.

This chapter does not present a mathematical formula that will help you settle, once and for all, and with complete peace of mind, your rate. Instead, I've assembled some hard-won advice from others who have proved themselves to be very nimble players of the game. Heed their guidance, and your confidence will grow.

Deciding your rate

Alina Wheeler, who shared advice in the previous chapter and who has many more years of design experience than I do, told me that pricing a job is quite simply a torturous and inefficient task for many design firms. "There are no magic formulas and there are no ultimate right numbers. What is a $25,000 US project for one client may actually be a $100,000 US project for another."

Many years ago, Alina had a design office called Katz Wheeler. To decide on a price, she and her partner, Joel Katz, would sit at a table and each write on a separate piece of

paper what they thought the job was worth. They'd fold their own piece of paper and slide it across the table to each other.

"We would always decide on a number that was between the two. It worked because we understood our overhead and we knew what profit margins we wanted. We tracked all jobs carefully, and knew at the end of a job how much time it took with a good client and how much time it took with a disorganized client. Our terms and conditions were clear, in terms of the scope of the engagement. The system worked."

You might not have a partner to swap prices with, or the experience Alina had amassed at that stage of her career, but you will have peers you can ask for help, whether it's designers you've subcontracted work to, previous employers, or people you've met through your blog. We all need help from time to time, so don't be afraid to ask.

Artificially inflating or deflating your rate usually backfires. For instance, whenever Alina didn't want to work on a particular project, she would put a really high price on it, thinking that it was a sure way to not get the job. "I always would get those jobs. I am certain that you have a similar story," she says.

The opposite direction is equally as unwise, Alina notes, perhaps more so because you also drag down others. "When you lowball a job to 'get it,' you are doing a disservice to yourself, your profession, and your client. You never, ever want to be perceived as the low-cost alternative."

Breaking down the proposal

Alina related to me how she creates a client proposal.

"I begin a proposal with the three major goals of the engagement. I use the same process diagram, and I add three deliverables for each of the five phases, along with a fee for each phase. A deliverable can be anything from a meeting to a design strategy. Since I have deconstructed each phase into a series of tasks, it is easy to estimate an isolated task. I end with three reasons why the client should work with me. For the contract, I use the same process with the deliverables and price, and I add terms and conditions. I make sure that I have clearly articulated what the client is responsible for. I know, for example, that when I have a single contact who is responsible for scheduling all meetings and gathering all information, that it will be an efficient process. I also know that when decision-makers are added later on, the process will be less successful."

Alina's system works because it is simple, logical, and streamlined. It respects the fact that most clients are overwhelmed with information and frequently receive voluminous proposals. "Clients rarely understand the differences and subtle nuances between design firms and their portfolios, or what it takes to create something really stellar, sustainable, and differentiated. But they understand process."

Another tip: It will help your clients understand what they're paying for if you separate your cost into categories. And if your proposal document is multiple pages, put the cost at the front. Anything you do to make it easier for the client to understand the way you will work together can only help you seal the deal and initiate a successful project. (We'll take a closer look at terms and conditions in the next chapter.)

It's not always about the money

When Ivan Chermayeff and Tom Geismar started their design practice in the late 1950s, one of the first things they did whenever possible was to trade design for some minor services they needed. Ivan cites the following example.

"When the time came to have an attorney to help with a simple contract agreement, we traded the legal fee for a letterhead design. We did such trades from time to time with landlords and other suppliers to whom we owed something— anyone who could use a little graphic design and didn't have anything of any quality in place."

Ivan isn't the only professional who has traded design for something else of value. Vancouver-based Nancy Wu recounts an occasion when she traded her design skills with a man who specialized in custom woodwork and home renovations.

"He asked if I ever traded services, as he needed some design work done and wondered if I needed anything done around the house. In fact, I did. I live in an old house with splintered wood in one spot, so I traded for minor work redoing the floors in my son's room, fixing some bathroom tile cracks, and creating a removable cover for one of the vents to keep the house warm during the winter months. In return, I designed a postcard, banner, and business card for an upcoming trade show. Our form of trade was less about monetary figures and more about value for value. He had one of his experienced men come in to put in new high quality laminate, taking advantage of the kind of discount rates they could obtain with their suppliers. Likewise, I had my own printing contacts and signage suppliers to help keep things affordable and on schedule to meet his deadline.

"In the end, it was a win-win situation and we ended up both being quite happy with the results. The key is that we kept it professional at the start, getting everything outlined in detail so that each of us knew what was needed and what the expected outcomes were."

Enter Mr. Procurement

Seattle-based management consultant Ted Leonhardt is experienced in helping creative firms become more effective in business. He told me about a particular designer he coached in order to get him to feel as bold as he acted in the following story (for the sake of the story we'll call the designer Ian). Ian led a team that designed the packaging for his client's most successful brand (we'll call the brand "Z"). The packaging resulted in sales of a billion dollars a year. But here Ian was, three years later, responding to a Request for Proposal (RFP) from the same company, the same team, even the same individuals.

"What's with these people?" Ian asked. "Don't they remember the success we had with the Z launch? We knocked it out of the park, and now they throw us into a competitive situation with an RFP."

Ted explained that most companies' procurement processes have an amped-up focus on negotiating every purchase, from machine tools to office supplies. Creative services are no exception. Ian's client now requires bids from three qualified suppliers for any purchase over $100K. Ian was lucky that he wasn't required to submit a Request for Qualification (RFQ) before submitting his RFP.

"Some call this the Walmart effect," Ted continues, "because of the relentless pursuit of the lowest costs, but it was the burst of the housing bubble in 2008 that really accelerated it. Consumers stopped consuming, and corporations tightened their belts. Today, purchasing agents and procurement departments have more influence than ever before. And it works! Employment is still off, but corporate profits are high, largely due to cost control."

According to Ted, Mr. Procurement exists for one reason only: to get the most while paying the least.

Recalling his meeting, Ian said, "There I was responding to Mr. Procurement's challenge of every line in our proposal with my heart pounding and two competitors standing in the wings. I reminded them of the success of the Z launch and Mr. P said, 'With all due respect I must remind you that there were many other factors in that success.'" Ted knows this is a classic intimidation technique meant to undermine Ian's confidence—Mr. P is a trained negotiator, and has many such techniques ready to use.

But Ian wasn't intimidated. "Of course, there were other factors," he replied. "But, please tell me why you would choose anyone else for the most critical factor of all, the creation of your consumer face? And, why would you cut the budget? Don't you know that those cuts will reduce the potential for success? Do you want us to do less discovery? Less strategy? Should we cut the research? Limit the creative time? Cut the rapid prototyping? On the shelf, on the site, and in the ads, your market will see only one thing: the package. Are you prepared to risk it all on someone who's not a proven winner? You represent a multi-billion-dollar corporation. This new launch has the potential to drop hundreds of millions to your bottom line. Are you prepared to risk that for a few hundred thousand in fees?"

There was a long pause.

The client team asked for 15 minutes alone. When they reassembled, Mr. Procurement compromised, and Ian compromised. A little.

Later, Ian's client said that Mr. Procurement was impressed with Ian, and that his comments had made sense—this was not a project to risk. Ian had asked for and received the respect he deserved. He did so by asking questions that reinforced his expertise and by explaining the consequences of cost cutting.

How to negotiate up

When you think of adjusting your fee during client discussions, chances are you'll think of a downward movement. But that shouldn't always be the case.

A prominent design company offered Krakow-based designer Andrea Austoni an ongoing collaboration. After the company accepted Andrea's hourly rate, he received the contract. There was a catch: Andrea wouldn't be able to mention this high-profile collaboration in his résumé and couldn't include any of the work in his portfolio. This changed the value of the transaction downward for the designer, so he raised the previously agreed-upon hourly rate, and after some time, the design company agreed with the request.

Andrea learned a few lessons from the experience. "Know your value and adjust your rates according to how much you stand to gain from a job in terms of exposure, portfolio building, and personal marketing value. Stand your ground."

Raising rates with existing clients

As I specialize in brand identity design, it means that most of my client projects are one-time jobs, with a high rate of client turnover, so I've not needed to raise my rates with an existing client. But if you're responsible for website development or marketing promotions, for instance, then it's almost inevitable that you will.

Karishma Kasabia, who shared a great marketing story in chapter 11, told me about how she handles the potentially difficult situation of raising her rates with existing clients.

"When we started the business, I was a freelancer working from home. Within two years, our expenses grew from home to office to studio, from freelancer to one designer, a second, a third, and then a manager."

Needless to say, it was vital that Karishma steadily introduce new rates along the way.

"I spoke to a few close clients to get their thoughts on this. Making good clients my friends has been one of the wisest things I've ever done."

The feedback she got covered two main points:

- Clients could allow for a 5 to 10 percent increase in the hourly rate when Karishma had moved from home to office.

- Clients thought it would be great if the increase was explained because they would feel included and be more receptive.

"So I spun the thought and designed an e-newsletter," she says. "It told current clients that their rate would stay the same for the next three months and would then graduate to a slightly higher rate."

The text read something like:

2008
No office.
No coffee.
Pixie cut.

2010
Office with air conditioning.
Coffee and sushi.
Bob cut.

"New clients would start at an even higher rate. I was giving the love to our existing clients and appreciating their loyalty," she adds. Also, any existing estimates would be valid for a longer period of time as well.

"Giving them time to adjust and celebrate our growth meant I dealt with no complaints at all."

"You should be charging more"

Surrey-based copywriter Mike Reed went freelance after previously founding a small agency called Other, where he worked as creative director. It didn't take Mike long to get freelance work from long-standing contacts, and he knew what he wanted to do in the longer term: work with the best branding and graphic design consultancies around.

"I wrote, and, I confess, designed a mailshot, which was a set of postcards each bearing an obscure word from the *Oxford English Dictionary*. 'Absquatuluate,' 'bathykolpian,' 'fanfaronade,' that sort of thing. These were 'free introductory words' for my targets, with the promise of more exciting language in exchange for money.

"Anyway, it worked. I got in to see a few of my favorite design consultancies, Hat-trick and The Partners first, as I recall, and it went from there.

"But one of the real bugbears was how much I should charge. I'd never been freelance before. How do you decide what rate you should be charging?"

Mike set a rate that seemed about right compared to the freelance design rates he'd been charged at his previous company, and off he went.

"Everyone was happy to pay what I was asking. As I recall, it was £350 per day, in 2002. I bumbled along like that, without much idea of how my rates compared to others', or of ways to find out. I can't remember why, but at some point I decided I was probably undercharging. I'd been going for a couple of years, so that was probably part of it: one feels one's income ought to go up a little each year, at least to account for inflation."

The new rate was tested when Mike tentatively announced it to one of his original freelance clients. They got on well, so he felt reasonably confident that if she thought it was an outrageous demand it wouldn't actually kill the relationship. Mike braced himself before explaining the new rate, but then couldn't believe his client's reply. "I've been meaning to say something," she said, "because I feel bad about what we're paying you. You should be charging more."

Mike recovered his composure and boldly suggested a *new* new rate. "A little higher," she suggested. Boggling at this, Mike followed her advice, and they agreed on a final figure.

"It was the most generous advice any client has ever given me, especially as it was her own business—and therefore her own money she was spending. Of course, the real issue was that I was undercharging considerably compared to the market, but she was under no obligation at all to reveal that."

That conversation didn't just transform Mike's income, it made him more confident about his work and how he dealt with clients. And you can imagine how fiercely loyal he was to that particular client from then on.

"It's still hard to make the jump to a new rate. You suddenly feel like maybe you'll scare the horses and end up with no clients. In my experience, that doesn't happen. The worst that can happen is that someone says, 'No, that's ridiculously high.' I haven't pushed hard enough for anyone to say that yet.

"My theory is that when you reach a point where people are consistently saying, 'That's a bit more than we're used to, is there any flexibility?' then I think you've got it about right."

Regardless of how many people you ask for help setting your rates, a huge factor is the confidence you have in your talent. Remember, clients will be looking for designers who present themselves as solid, reputable, talented, experienced, trustworthy, and passionate about the profession—designers just like you. These traits take years to nurture and shouldn't come cheap: good clients understand that. So when it comes to sending that quote, always ask yourself if you've set the bar high enough.

Chapter 17

TERMS AND CONDITIONS

In the early years of my self-employment, getting things in writing wasn't too much of a concern. I was keener to make things as easy as possible for my client, not wanting to add the burden of paperwork and signatures.

But then came those inevitable projects when I was expected to go far above and beyond the original scope of the project. Those situations arose because there were no specific terms and conditions, no definite deliverables that had been signed off on.

On one occasion, a client of mine kept sending revision requests. The "orders" were arriving on an almost daily basis for weeks on end until it was clear there was no way I could create something he'd be happy with. In addition, the time I'd already spent on the project had eaten all my profits.

These situations can be avoided by putting in place a definite set of project guidelines—something for the client to sign at the outset. Should the project run off course, you'll have documentation that will protect you.

Pear Deli and the sword of Damocles

Oregon-based designer Von Glitschka learned the contract lesson the hard way. (Names in the following story have been changed.)

In 2007, he was subcontracted to work with a small creative firm based in New York City. Whenever the firm needed a logo, icons, illustration, or whatever, it would commission Von. He worked with the firm's creative director Irvin for about a year on various projects until Irvin left the agency and took a new job as an in-house creative director for a New York City chain of grocery stores called Pear Deli.

"In late 2008, Irvin wanted to hire me to create a set of 45 food icons for use on Pear Deli's in-store signage throughout all their locations," Von said. "I sent a quote for the project and Irvin approved it. Because I had worked with him before, I didn't request a signature or bother with a contract. Everything was approved via email or verbally over the phone."

Von created the illustration set then delivered the final art, invoicing that October. In January of 2009, he received an email from Irvin asking if he could create two more pieces of art to complete the set. Von agreed and told Irvin he'd just send another invoice for the two additional pieces along with the final art. Irvin agreed.

"After another month had passed I realized the original invoice was over 90 days old," said Von, "so I sent Irvin an email but never heard back. A few weeks later I sent another, still no reply. At this time I was busy with other work and another month went by and still no payment. I decided to call Pear Deli and talk to Irvin directly."

But Von found out that Irvin no longer worked for the company, so he asked to talk to accounts payable and was transferred to someone else. That person told him there was no invoice and requested that he email it to him directly, which Von did.

"I didn't hear back that week," Von said, "so I sent a follow-up email and got no response. I called and left a message with Pear Deli accounts payable and still nothing. Another month went by and I was able to talk to someone else at Pear Deli. They told me they didn't have any record of me doing any work for them and refused to process my invoice."

During the next several days, Von tracked down Irvin and asked him to call Pear Deli and straighten the situation out so Von could get paid for the work he did, work that totaled more than $4,000. Irvin gave Von the owner's contact information at Pear Deli but repeated attempts by email and phone proved useless. At this point it was about eight months after Von had sent the initial invoice, and he was frustrated. He was getting the runaround and decided to send the invoice to a collections agency to at least recoup something rather than nothing.

"I discovered that I couldn't collect from out-of-state due to some New York City law and that I had to hire a New York City collection agency to do it on my behalf," he said. "There was one just down the street from Pear Deli headquarters, and they agreed to collect for me."

Another two months went by and the collection agency couldn't get Pear Deli to pay. The agency said the only way to get the money was to file a legal claim with the local court. This cost $95, and the agency would handle things from there. Von agreed, and the legal claim was filed. At that point it was September of 2009.

In January of 2010, after three more months and still no collection, Von received a letter from Pear Deli's attorney notifying him that they were suing for $250,000 accusing Von of harassment and extortion. The paperwork stated that Von had no claim to the money he was trying to collect because Pear Deli never hired him.

"At this point," said Von, "I was just shocked. How was this possible? I created the art, I delivered the art, the person I worked with knows I did, yet they're saying none of it was true? I once again contacted Irvin and asked him if he could go on record to confirm I created the art for Pear Deli while he was the creative director. He said he didn't want to get involved in the situation.

"I talked to my business lawyer locally, and he summed up the letter as an intimidation ploy. Pear Deli had a far deeper wallet than I did, so they decided it was worth scaring me rather than paying what they owed. My lawyer got on my case for not having a proper contract, and we agreed to write one I could use moving forward.

"Since the legal letter came from a New York City jurisdiction, my lawyer couldn't respond to it, and I had to use the collection agency's lawyer, who thankfully said he'd make them go away by stating I'd drop my claim for collection. Even though I dropped my claim it really pissed me off that a business would do this to me. The whole experience was kind of surreal, and I was mad at myself for letting it happen."

The next day Von talked to one of his designer friends in New York City, who agreed to stop by one of the Pear Deli locations to have a look at the signage. That same day Von received an email from his friend with three attachments, each showing in-store signage at Pear Deli using Von's artwork.

"It was like getting salt rubbed into an open wound," Von said. "All kinds of thoughts cascaded through my conscience. How could this happen? How could someone just flat-out lie like this and think it was OK? I was pissed, but I also felt vulnerable. I didn't want to kick a hornet's nest that had no problem hanging a $250,000 sword of Damocles over my head. I had no contractual leverage, and I knew that was the real problem.

"I contacted my copyright lawyer to see if I could handle it from that angle, but it would have ended up costing more than what they owed me just to pursue it, with no guarantee whatsoever. I was not happy how any of this came out but I decided to live and learn and just drop it all.

"Over the next several months, I worked out a contract form for my business that I now use with clients. I prefer the term 'work agreement' instead of 'contract.' It just sounds more approachable and doesn't come with any preconceived baggage like 'contract' tends to paint in people's minds. When I work with large ad agencies, I'm usually signing their contract. When I work with smaller firms or business owners I use my form.

"Having a custom contract written for your business will cost you anywhere from $500 to $1,500 or more in legal fees to have a lawyer spend the necessary time to finesse it for your specific needs. But don't think of it as an expense. It's an investment worth its weight in gold in terms of protecting you from those who have no integrity and would seek to exploit your work for their gain at your expense."

Growing pains

When Jonathan Selikoff first started his New York-based design studio, Selikoff+Company, most of his work and income were generated from work for other design agencies. Jonathan's goal was to eventually shed this work by building a base of clients to grow with, handling the creation of their brands, and managing their growth.

"Lucky for me," said Jonathan, "a client materialized from a posting on an online message board looking for someone to design an identity and packaging for a new health-care product. I wrote a proposal, drafted a creative brief, and followed all of the steps I should have, except for sending the prospect a written contract. Looking back, I was so happy for the opportunity to bring on the type of client I was looking for—a new company with a great idea and a strong vision for what they wanted their brand to become—that I overlooked the risk inherent in the launch of a new company."

Jonathan's client achieved nationwide distribution for its product, largely based on the client's strong identity and packaging (which stood out in a rapidly expanding category). As the company grew, it needed to produce more materials: catalogs, sell sheets, a website, and advertisements. So the two parties began a retainer-based relationship. The rapid growth continued, and the client launched new products, expanded into other national retailers, and had an active trade show program that kept Jonathan busy and growing right along with them.

"Sounds like a dream, right?" Jonathan said. "Unfortunately, the company didn't have the financing to support its rapid growth and had difficulties both producing enough products and supporting them with consistent marketing. Cash flow issues arose, we were lax with our collections, and eventually the company owed us for a considerable amount of work. With no contract, we couldn't prove the terms under which we'd been working with them, leaving us without the option of pursuing legal action."

Fortunately for Jonathan, the founders were honest people who have been paying him little by little. He designed a new product launch in the midst of this issue, but this time required a 50 percent deposit on the project. He also didn't release final files until the remainder of the project was paid. This new project was, of course, specified on paper in the form of a signed proposal.

"We still have a good relationship with the company and its founders," said Jonathan, "but we learned several important lessons that many start-up design firms have also learned the hard way: always have a contract, monitor the state of the business, and when payment slows or stops, don't keep working based on promises."

What to include

With the help of some close allies in the profession, I've tailored a set of terms and conditions that I need all clients to agree to before I'll begin any work on their projects. A document containing the information is emailed to my clients, with space for their signature and the date at the bottom.

You might encounter a client who wants to change your terms. This happened to me on one particular occasion, and I don't think it was a coincidence that I never received full payment upon completion (not because of the new terms, but because of a difficult client who may never have had any intention to pay in full). That project taught me to view any amendment request as a red flag.

You're welcome to use the following terms as is or edit them for your own purposes. It's also wise to consult with an attorney to make sure your terms and conditions will work for you.

Rights and ownership

Rights: All services provided by the designer shall be for the exclusive use of the client other than for the designer's promotional use. Upon payment of all fees and expenses, the following reproduction rights for all approved final designs created by the designer for this project shall be granted:

Client to gain full transferable rights to brand identity.

Client to gain full license to reproduce works through commercial printers.

Ownership: The client shall be entitled to full ownership of all artwork created during the project upon full payment of the agreed fee.

Third-party contracts: The designer may contract with other creative professionals to provide services such as web development, photography, and illustration. Any third-party terms and conditions will include full reproduction rights for the client. Where such contracting adds to the project cost, the client will first be asked for permission to proceed. No project will commence on the assumption that third parties *might* be required for project completion. Such details will be finalized prior to project commencement, unless requested by the client at a later date.

Communication

The designer can be reached by telephone from Monday to Friday between 9 a.m. and 5 p.m. GMT. Skype chats are welcomed. The majority of designer/client communication is normally via email, helping both parties keep track of specific design requirements and potential changes.

Payment schedule

The client will make a 50 percent down payment prior to work commencing. The project can be scheduled once the down payment is received by the designer. The down payment is nonrefundable. The remaining 50 percent is payable to the designer upon completion of the project and before original artwork is supplied to the client.

Delayed payment

If the final invoice is not paid within 30 days, a 5 percent "delayed payment" fee will be charged. This initial 5 percent figure will be added upon each recurring 30-day period until the full amount has been received by the designer.

Cancellation

If, after project commencement, client communication (face-to-face, telephone, or email) stops for a period of 180 days, the project can be cancelled, in writing by the designer, and ownership of all copyrights shall be retained by the designer. A cancellation fee for work completed shall be paid by the client, with the fee based on the stage of project completion. The fee will not exceed 110 percent of the total project cost.

Miscellaneous

Samples: The client shall provide the designer with samples of print design that result from the project deliverables. Such samples shall be representative of the highest quality of work produced. The designer may use such copies and samples for publication, exhibition, or other promotional purposes.

The designer shall have the right to photograph all completed designs or installations and shall have the right to use such photographs for publication, exhibition, or other promotional purposes.

Confidentiality: The client shall inform the designer in writing before the project commences if any portion of any material or information provided by the client or if any portion of the project is confidential.

Indemnity: The client agrees to indemnify and hold harmless the designer from any and all claims, demands, losses, causes of action, damage, lawsuits, judgments, including attorneys' fees and costs, but only to the extent caused by, arising out of, the work supplied by the designer.

It's not unusual

San Francisco-based designer Ian Vadas is another who recommends including a cancellation fee (or kill fee)—a clause in your contract that says if the client terminates the project midway through, then a fee to "kill" the contract must be made. Ian recently worked on a project where this issue came up.

"The client decided to back out of the project after about 80 percent of the work was done," said Ian. "I had the initial 50 percent deposit, and kept it, but lost out on time for the work I had already completed, plus the remaining amount to finish the project. If I had included a kill fee in my contract, it might have convinced the client to see the project through."

Houston-based graphic artist Patricia Schaefer learned early on to always require 50 percent up front for design services.

"Clients who balk at a down payment for creative work are usually those who won't pay you at all," said Patricia. "I've learned this the hard way, particularly from clients who were friends, either personally or professionally. They tell you that other designers don't make them pay up front, or they are offended that you don't trust them. If they want you, they'll pay, and standing your ground is much better than caving in and finding your ideas being implemented by your client, or another designer, without you seeing a dime. Trust me, I've been there."

Another practice that Patricia has learned the importance of—and one I highlight in the "ownership" section of my terms and conditions—is to stipulate that all design is copyrighted under her until the work has been paid for in full. It adds an extra incentive for clients to pay quickly so they can use the new creative without issue.

One incident that Patricia remembers from early in her career is when she sketched a rough idea for a bumper sticker for a radio station. She was asked to submit a design, and sketched it on some scrap paper right then and there, presenting it to the program director. "I was promised payment, but what was I thinking?" Patricia asked herself. "The next thing I know there are all these bright and shiny newly printed bumper stickers out there with my rough sketch on them, to size, in neon green and yellow, on clear Mylar no less. The worst thing was that everyone was complaining to me about the quality of my artwork! It was a rough sketch, an idea, a proof, not anywhere close to the final design I had planned to flesh out. And I certainly would not have recommended those colors on that material."

Patricia learned two important things from just that one incident: Get some form of payment up front, and get all the information up front, too, including print details (in order to offer advice if necessary).

In more than 15 years in business, only one of Patricia's potential clients has ever refused to do business with her because of her 50 percent up front rule.

"I'm very much against spec work of almost any kind," Patricia said. "We all have our instances where we will do pro bono work for one reason or another, but even the smallest charity can often barter for design work—even if it is just advertising you through their social networks or naming you as a contributing sponsor on their promotions. Selling yourself short happens, but don't give yourself away completely for free, ever."

Ultimately, incorporating terms and conditions into your workflow is as much about ensuring that your clients know exactly what they're getting as it is what they're *not* getting for their money. For example, if you're creating a website, are you also handling site updates? If not, you should say this in your terms so there's no uncertainty when a client requests a tiny change (a lot of tiny changes will lead to a lot of your time).

We'll end this chapter with a few final words from Von Glitschka:

"Whether you call it a contract, a work agreement, or just itemize the deliverables on a provided quote and have the client sign off on it to green-light the project, the point is to have a mutual understanding and clear communication between you and your client as to what you are being hired to create, how much they'll pay you to create it, and who owns the final product when it's done."

Chapter 18

HOW TO BEST PRESENT YOUR WORK

It doesn't matter if the design you've created can't possibly be bettered. If you don't present it to your client in a way that captivates the imagination, you have increased the chance that your client will just say no.

Contrary to what many believe, good design doesn't sell itself. You need to show your client you studied and understood the client's problem, then communicate your solution in an appropriate manner.

There's some important advice I want to share about best practice in design presentation, advice you can immediately use in your own client projects.

Listen and build rapport

Eric Karjaluoto of smashLAB (who shared advice in chapter 12) trained as an artist, not as a designer. Part of that training involved not only coming up with and executing ideas, but also learning how to defend them. This last point was notably important: in an art school environment, your ability to think critically and articulate a perspective often carries as much weight as the work itself. So although the art was presented in its final state, without the capacity for change, Eric still needed to defend what he created, putting him in the habit of defending all artistic decisions. A designer, on the other hand, must be ready to listen and adjust the work as necessary.

Coupled with a rather staunch work ethic, this made Eric's first years as a designer more difficult than they needed to be. "I worked my ass off to make a project as good as possible, and then I'd prepare for 'battle,' should the client not be immediately comfortable with the proposed design approach," he said.

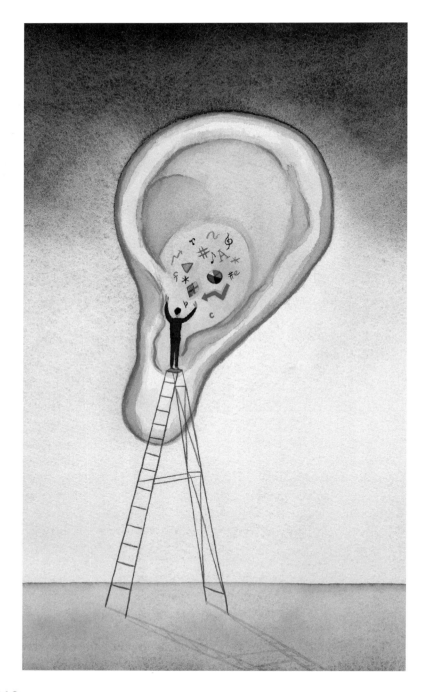

Eric rightly believed that it was his duty to challenge ideas that would stand between his clients and their stated goals. But he mistakenly put too much emphasis on the finished product, thinking that the journey was simply a means to an end. In reality, it's the journey that keeps the client on board, vital for helping reach consensus when the finished design is showcased.

This was perhaps most evident when he was working with a client who was a nice person, but who had some strange ideas surrounding design. "The engagement started well," he said, "with a lot of positive discussion around strategy. From there, matters devolved. Relations became a little tense during the information architecture stage, so by the time creative rolled around, the engagement was incredibly strained. All of the fun was gone, and we were left trying to make the best of a crummy situation.

"I have to stress that this client's requests were, at times, highly impractical," Eric added. "For example, he asked us to keep the text large, variable in length, but never require scrolling—a nice idea, but largely a physical impossibility."

While such requests were confounding, the way Eric chose to respond didn't make things better. Eric was so focused on showing that his way was right that he failed to properly lead the client, and his company, through the process. The job did finally come to an end, and the results were acceptable. But it couldn't be called a fun experience.

"The bummer was that everyone felt beat by it—both on the client side and at our agency," Eric added. "I didn't expect they'd ever work with us again, and I certainly didn't feel like working for them again. This seemed like an unacceptable end. It conflicted with my view of what our company offered customers."

Eric resolved that he needed to rethink the way that he and his agency worked with clients.

"Imagine walking into a store in which you are asked to drop several thousand dollars," he said, "without even knowing what you'd be left with. Then ask how you'd feel if you voiced a concern, only to have the sales rep sigh and say, 'No, you're wrong. Trust me. I've done this hundreds of times before. I'll take care of you.'

"This isn't that far from how I'd been treating my clients," Eric said. "They'd enter a process that likely felt quite nebulous, and I'd just retreat to the lab and get down to solving the problem at hand. I'd run through myriad variations, but I didn't include them in this process. Upon presenting the work, I didn't really want to be challenged by irrelevant points. I'd also get cranky if they asked their friends for opinions or tried to 'help' by contributing their own design ideas.

"Sure, the design solution is important, but it's not everything. There's simply more to what we do than the files that are delivered at the project's end. It's a relationship, a dialogue, and something that requires trust. As a result, we need to facilitate appropriate design solutions through an experience that our customers find accessible, pleasurable, and rewarding," Eric said.

"This means slowing down, explaining notions that might seem obvious to us as professionals, really listening to client concerns, entertaining odd change requests, and—perhaps more than anything—explaining our thoughts carefully, instead of just defending them. We aren't artists; our creativity is only one part of the value we afford our clients.

"The way we interact," added Eric, "how our clients feel about the process, and the comfort built as a result of having established a good rapport are all central to being a design professional. We put a lot of time into designing work; we need to place an equal priority on designing a brilliant customer experience for those who trust us with their brands.

"Ease up on your clients," advised Eric. "The end result is that it will get easier for you, too."

Guide your client

John Clifford of New York-based Think Studio had a particular client who seemed to have a sophisticated sense of design. Trusting that sense, John didn't feel the need to explain his ideas. But he soon realized his client always chose the safest option, which was usually not the most effective. "I then understood I needed to explain why and how the design solved his problem, and why one direction was stronger than another," said John. "It also put the two of us in a position of discussing the design, rather than the client dictating how it should be and what needs to be changed."

This is a lesson that I also learned the hard way, having worked through quite a number of projects before I realized my mistake: I wasn't making a strong verbal case in favor of the work. Sure, my designs might have looked the part, but very few clients will have your sense of artistic vision or completely understand all of the content you've put into a design. So unless you talk them through the idea, all of that work is likely to go unnoticed.

Avoid the disparate client

Turkey-based graphic designer Atakan Seçkin recalls an instance when he actually ended a client relationship after the client was unable to choose from his options.

"I was contacted by a local solar energy company and asked to renew its brand identity," said Atakan. "My client and I scheduled regular meetings with the participation of the owner and three members of the management board.

"After providing my initial concepts, the board told me that its members loved the outcome, but needed some time to think. A couple of weeks later, I was told they couldn't decide because they each voted for different designs. They said they could decide easily if they saw *the one*."

So Atakan kept on designing and provided new ideas. His client took more time to think. But still there was no decision.

"Then I understood that the problem was not the quality of designs," explained Atakan, "it was the diversity between their minds, the way each of them thought about the company."

That was not a problem he could solve. The project was unsuccessful, and Atakan and his client parted company.

It's an example of what can happen when each member of the committee isn't pulling in the same direction, and a reminder of the importance of the initial questions you ask your client (questions we covered in chapter 15). If you can discern this disunity early, you will save yourself time and aggravation. Be prepared to direct your client's attention back to the design brief if you think the process is running off course. Your ideas will, after all, relate specifically to the answers your client provided at the outset. Sometimes it can be important to remind the committee of this.

I remember a few past projects when immediately after my presentation, the clients said my ideas were excellent, but after a few days passed, doubt began to set in and changes were requested, usually resulting in a less risky, but much weaker outcome. If the committees were in agreement about the proposed new direction from the outset, such projects could've been much more successful.

Too many ideas

One of my first projects in self-employment was to create a logo for a South African Web hosting company called Circle. In my eagerness to please when my initial ideas weren't accepted, I suggested that I publish a blog post showing all my sketches, inviting readers to share their thoughts. I was at a stage in learning where I didn't understand the downside of simply showing and sharing too much. My sketches were online for anyone to see and comment on. This meant my client was reading the opinion of people who would never use his service, and who might not have had any valuable design experience from which to make an informed comment.

Here's what I learned:

1. It's never a good move to show all of your ideas. There will inevitably be poor ones in the mix. Lest we forget the influence of Sod's Law (or Murphy's Law, for my American audience), if you show a client ten ideas (nine good, one bad) the odds on the bad idea being chosen are significantly shorter than 10 to 1. It's closer to a coin toss. Whittle it down: Only show your best work.

2. When you present your client with too many options, the task of choosing becomes much more difficult. It's much easier to choose one from two samples, rather than one from 50.

3. Inviting the general public to pass judgment (on a blog or otherwise) disregards your client's target audience. Also, many who offer comments are unlikely to have any notable design experience. When your client reads the comments, that throws a further spanner in the works.

Any one of these mistakes would be enough to hinder a project's completion, let alone all three combined. Needless to say, I never did finish that logo.

Concentrate on the big goals

It's part of your job to keep everyone focused on the big picture and not on the micro-details that can derail a presentation. John Clifford shared a client meeting in which he inadvertently threw everyone off track.

"As I was wrapping up the presentation I made the mistake of asking the vague question, 'What do you think?'" said John. "After some silence, a committee member said, 'Mmm... I don't really like yellow.' Then another agreed, 'I don't like yellow either!' Someone else chimed in with, 'I like yellow okay, but it reminds me of our house color before we painted it.'

"I stood there, a bit dumbfounded, as people started talking about house colors they liked and didn't like," said John. "Nobody was talking about the project. To rein them in, I had to interrupt and bring us back to the work. I told the committee that we could get into detail like colors later in the project, but that we needed to talk about the overall concept. I said something like, 'The main goal is to give your company a recognizable and unique look, while speaking to your target market more directly. The structure and language shown here address this in a smart, fun way. Do you agree?' That way, everyone could keep in mind why the meeting was taking place and what we were trying to accomplish. Clients don't need to personally *like* it—though I hope they love it—but the solution has to *work*. Concentrate on the goals."

Show your work in context

Here's a relevant case study from Chermayeff & Geismar's 2011 book *Identify* (Print Publishing, 2011). When Giorgio Armani was first shown Chermayeff & Geismar's new logo for Armani Exchange (A|X), he rejected it outright. The designers later found out that due to Armani's infamously busy schedule, the new mark had been presented to him between meetings, on a white piece of paper. The A|X directors of advertising and branding, Tom Jarrold and Matthew Scrivens, then suggested approaching Armani a second time (which they almost never do) with the entire Chermayeff & Geismar presentation, which showed the logo in such applications as magazine ads, storefronts, and billboards. Once Armani saw the increased visual impact of the new identity in context, he immediately approved it.

Embrace feedback

To be successful, all design projects need more than a designer. They also need the client's input.

Early in his career, Jerry Kuyper (a Connecticut-based designer whose clients have included AT&T, Santander, GE, World Wildlife Fund, and many others) resisted most feedback from clients. "After all," he said, "how could a client possibly see something I hadn't already considered?" Occasionally, though, upon reviewing the work six months later, Jerry would be hit by a bolt of objectivity and decide the client had been absolutely right.

"Over time," said Jerry, "I have moved to a position where I accept any and all client or partner suggestions by replying, 'Interesting. I'll have a look at that.' Two things happen: first, the client feels heard and included in the process, and second, they trust me when I show and explain why their request does or doesn't work. The key is translating the specifics of what the client is requesting to an understanding of what they are trying to achieve."

A few years ago, Jerry had a client enthusiastically select a logo. The client then proceeded to give Jerry many directions on refinement. More than 140 variations were created after the initial logo was selected, and Jerry spent more time designing those variations than he did the initial exploration.

"A few suggestions were so bad," Jerry said, "I would have denied any involvement if one had been selected, over my protests. Amazingly, one of the worst ideas did open up an avenue I hadn't explored and led to a breakthrough. I don't think I would have ever reached that solution without being open to my client's approach."

The lesson learned?

"Don't be too attached to your work," advises Jerry, "and trust your clients; they can take you to some interesting places."

How clients can be rude, but right

Nick Asbury, of England-based creative partnership Asbury & Asbury, was working on a brand book for a big client. He was pleased with the first draft—creative, funny, unpretentious, not what you expect from a brand book. The client committee liked it, too, but started rowing back on the idea that had originally excited them.

"Over a period of weeks," said Nick, "there was a series of skirmishes as the more creative turns of phrase were replaced by safer alternatives. I won some battles, ceded ground on others. We arrived at a draft that I still thought was pretty good, albeit having lost some of the spirit of the original.

"Then the real client arrived. It turned out the feedback over the preceding weeks had been from the marketing manager, but the real person signing it off was the brand manager, who worked on another continent. He was one of the people who liked the original draft and now he was laying into this new version, complaining it had lost its spark," said Nick.

"The feedback was pretty rudely expressed: 'This part reads like a high-school essay,' and 'This bit feels like it could be from an annual report.' And the feedback came with an accompanying demand to have a new version within 24 hours, even though they'd dragged the process out for weeks to reach this point."

Nick's initial reaction was the usual mixture of wounded professional pride, irritation at the schedule, and personal affront at the tone of the feedback. He was close to putting all this in a late-night email and firing it off.

"But at those moments when you're most sure you're in the right," advised Nick, "it's always worth conducting a quick thought experiment: What if you're not? Once the initial personal reaction had died down, a voice in my head started asking whether the client might have a point. The tone of the feedback was annoying, but the content wasn't unreasonable. The 24-hour deadline was a headache, but it was do-able. The big picture was that we both thought the copy had lost something. Here was a client fighting to make something braver, not blander. It was a good thing."

Instead of writing that late-night email, Nick started rewriting the copy. After those weeks of gradual chipping away, he enjoyed rediscovering the spirit of his original work. And the result was an improvement—addressing a lot of the practical concerns the client had, but retaining the creative edge that made it different.

"For me," Nick said, "it was a reminder that it's always about the creative end product. The rest is process and personalities. Giving feedback is hard work—I've had to do it myself. It can come across as rude, when really you just don't have time to phrase it tactfully. As a seasoned creative, it's possible for cynicism to set in—you assume the client is always out to destroy your beautifully crafted work. But there are plenty of clients out there who believe in great work and want to make it happen as much as you do, sometimes more. When you find them, make sure you hold onto them. And don't send them emails late at night."

Presentation tips

Here are some final words from Think Studio's John Clifford, written for this book.

- **Prepare.** Don't wing it. Don't read from a script, but know the main points that need to be discussed. I remember a colleague who neglected to mention one of the key aspects of our concept. Without hearing it, the client had a tough time understanding the idea.

- **Be confident.** Know what you're talking about. You are the expert on the design of this project, so you need to convey some authority.

- **When speaking, end your statements with a period, not a question mark.** If your voice goes up at the end of each sentence, you sound like a child that needs approval. Designers looking for a job have spoken this way when presenting me with their work, and I find it very hard to imagine them in a meeting with any of my clients.

- **Be excited.** If you sound bored, everyone else will be bored too.

BEFORE WE DEPART

The preceding sections covered the most frequently asked questions I receive about starting and running a successful design business. But I didn't want to leave you with just that. The following pages contain questions that don't come up as often, but are well worth knowing the answers to.

I also wanted to leave you with some ideas on how to move away from client work and "automate" your earning potential—that is, how to earn passive income—as well as how to keep motivational "income" flowing in so that you remain creatively rich.

Chapter 19

THE MENTORS SPEAK

It's true that there's no faster way to learn than by doing it yourself, and the mistakes you're personally responsible for leave you much less likely to make the same one twice. That said, it's always good to receive advice from those who have already learned the lessons and suffered through the mistakes, especially when it's your business that's at stake.

For the purpose of this chapter, I talked to a variety of designers about their business experience and asked them to share advice specifically applicable to you—the design business owner.

Team up with different specialists

Ivan Chermayeff told me of a time when Eliot Noyes, a distinguished industrial designer/architect, obtained an assignment from Mobil Oil Corporation to modernize Mobil gasoline stations in the United States and abroad.

"When an architect or industrial designer, who has an established practice but without any graphic design capabilities, recognizes his or her limitations," said Chermayeff, "then one has a starting entry point. Such was the case with Eliot. He realized that his ability to develop an accompanying graphic identity for his client was not as focused as our talents in this important corollary role. So we joined forces. The result on his part was to develop the canopies and gas pumps. For our part, we moved the flying red horse off the main sign, made it red, and put it into a mascot position on the station's building. We emphasized the 'o' in Mobil, in a way that suggested a simple wheel inside a five-letter word, which supported the idea of movement and, by extension, transportation."

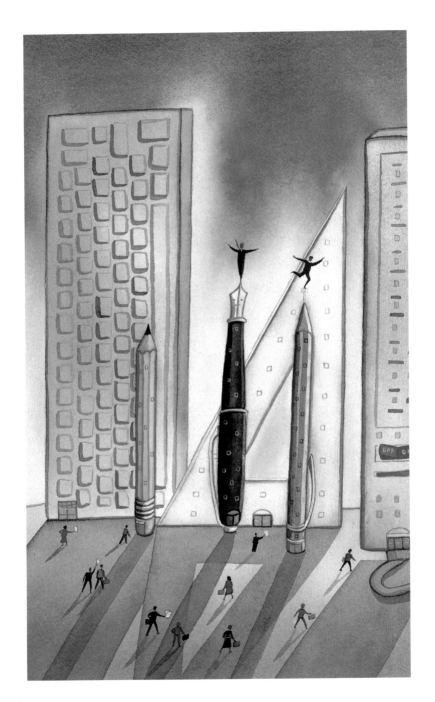

Wait until you're hired

It can be tempting to work on ideas before an agreement has been reached, but more often than not, it will lead to your prospect disappearing with some free work, never to be heard from again.

Alina Wheeler agrees. "I don't solve a problem until I am hired to solve a problem," said Alina. "It begins with the marketing. When I meet a prospective client, I first focus on listening. Then, I show a process diagram that is one page. I review the process that I will use to solve their problem. I talk about the kind of problems that I have solved, and articulate the value to the client. Every project I have ever worked on fits into the five phases of my process."

By focusing on how you do what you do, rather than actually doing it in advance, you're not only protecting yourself against time-wasters, but you're letting the client into your process and setting his or her mind at ease about allocating the design budget to you.

Your clients can help you grow

In 2009, an entrepreneur named Cherie Yvette came to Virginia-based designer Reese Spykerman with a proposal: take her existing art and branding, kick it up several notches, and work with her developers and artists to art direct a cohesive website design and print campaign.

In the three years since, Reese said she has become a better designer because of her work with Cherie.

"Cherie's provided me with some of the most detailed research and style preferences of any of our clients," said Reese. "She consistently references specific designs, physical products, websites and campaigns whose mood, feel, and typographic approach she'd like to emulate. She's organized, too, and puts them all into PDFs or PowerPoint presentations with detailed notes. But unlike some potential clients who ask us to copy another brand outright, which we never do, Cherie asks us to take all these pieces into consideration and make something new for her brand.

"Cherie exposes me to new typographical solutions, ways to layer texture, and restrained color palettes. Her specific direction doesn't delve into micromanagement; instead we've settled into the kind of client/designer flow that only comes after years of understanding each other's work styles and personalities," said Reese.

Collaboration with your clients can inspire you to push harder and to consider new solutions.

Don't limit creativity to your day job

"The ideal creative solution doesn't always involve typography or color palettes or a clever headline," says Jessica Hagy, a freelance copywriter and author of the popular blog *Indexed*.

"An artist can become a strategic guru," she explained. "Copywriters can sculpt. An account executive can be a curator. Junior associates can lead revolutions. Even Dr. Seuss was a copywriter once," added Jessica.

"Creativity need not stop at the boundary of your job description. Why do 'creatives' assume that their clients desperately need creative solutions in order to thrive, but neglect to apply such thinking to their own problems?

"A true creative applies creativity to more than just billable tasks," said Jessica. "A true creative sees every situation as an opportunity to make the world more livable, wonderful, and remarkable."

30 years of advice

London-based Mike Dempsey spent 30 years running Carroll, Dempsey & Thirkell, and after he moved on from the company (he's now trading as Studio Dempsey) Mike took time to share a few pearls of wisdom should you go on to expand your business:

1. Don't go into business with your best friends because it's highly likely that you'll lose them.

2. Never let the creative heart slip from the front of the company.

3. Take care in over-manning (and woman-ing).

4. Make sure that creatives always have contact with clients.

5. Choose your staff with care.

6. Watch out for cuckoos in the nest; they can destroy your world.

7. Always try to be fair and kind.

8. Listen to your financial advisors, but don't let them anywhere near the creative table. They have a different and often extremely devious headspace that is not compatible with designers.

9. Always seek out work that really interests you. You'll put more into it and do a far better job.

10. Don't get into the rut of working late every night. It's a killer.

11. Encourage everyone to soak up all of the other creative disciplines. Graphic design is not the only thing on the block; there's far more out there.

12. If you don't like the job you're in, leave it. Life is too short, and we only have one (although I have hopes).

Preparatory experience is key

I asked Jerry Kuyper what advice he'd give to those wanting to start their own business and he said:

"Gain solid experience with companies that do what you want to do. I worked for large, highly regarded brand identity firms for over 20 years before starting my own firm. It doesn't have to be 20 years.

"Be bold, believe in yourself, and expect to work long and hard, which, if you love what you do, isn't really work."

Ask for feedback about you

When a final design has been selected, and the project is completed, ask your client what he or she thought about working with you. Don't force it, because this is a favor to you, but if your client does share an insight it can benefit you in two ways:

1. You can improve any shortcomings you might have for the benefit of future clients.

2. You can use positive feedback to display on your website's testimonial page or alongside the portfolio piece, which will help to attract future clients.

Behavioral lessons

Prior to his tenure as digital design director for the *New York Times*, Khoi Vinh co-founded Behavior, a design studio in New York City, where he spent four years building the business. At the end of 2011, he took time to reflect on the lessons learned along the way, publishing his thoughts on his blog. He agreed to share his discoveries here, for you.

People

"Almost nothing matters more than people. How well a team works together, through good times and bad, day in and day out, is a bigger determining factor in building a successful business than the contracts you win, the work that you do, the press coverage you get, or even the money you make.

"The way to form a good team is to gather people of complementary talents and temperaments and unite them under a single vision," he explained. "By contrast, my former partners and I started our studio primarily because we were thrown together by circumstance: In the fall of 2001 and in the aftermath of 9/11, with no one hiring, we had almost no other choice but to form a company of our own. But our disparate attitudes, approaches, and visions for the business inevitably led to strife, and before too long I could no longer answer the question, 'Do you like working with these people?' with a 'yes.' If you're going to undertake the hard work of building a company, the answer to that question should always be a resounding 'yes.' Life is too short for it to be otherwise."

Clients

"You cannot succeed in design services unless you really believe in your clients and their products," Khoi said. "Just as it's essential to enjoy working with the people you form a company with, working with clients that you like is essential, too. I liked some of the clients I worked with, and I flatly disliked others.

"I did my best work for the former," he said, "and I did a disservice to the latter, most of whom had hired us to help further businesses that I felt no passion for, or was outright skeptical of. For years, I thought that my disinterest was immaterial, that I was such a talented designer that I could do a good job for anyone. But before long it became apparent to me that unless I was fully bought into a client's vision, my work would always be subpar. If you're trying to build a design studio based on a reputation for doing phenomenal work, taking on assignments from clients you don't believe in is a waste of everyone's time."

Client work versus products

"I've known lots of people," said Khoi, "who got into services thinking that they can use the income from clients to bankroll their own product ideas. That is not an impossible scenario—it's been done more than a few times before, and it's a beautiful thing when it happens. But it's very, very difficult to pull off. To do services, you need to wake up in the morning with a different approach to life from the way you wake up in the morning to do products, and only a few people have the skill—and stamina—to juggle both at once," he explained.

"If I were to start a new studio, I would square with myself, and my partners, that we'd be in the business of providing services to our clients, period. It's so hard to do a good job for clients, and so hard to build a sustainable business in client services, that I wouldn't want the creative and emotional distraction of trying to build products of our own, too."

Vision

"The funny thing about design services is that it's relatively easy to get started, but very tricky to make work," said Khoi. "Lots of companies need design help in some form, so if you win one or two clients—which is actually fairly easy to do—suddenly you have a business with real revenue. The really challenging part is whether you can turn a handful of jobs into a financially lucrative client roster that consistently brings you creatively satisfying work. That's a lot harder.

"What is required more than anything is vision—articulating your goals and creating a plan to achieve them," he added. "Even more important is to make sure that same vision is mutually held by all of your partners. It's hard to underestimate how valuable it is to agree, up front, on how big you want the company to grow, what kind of clients you want to win, how long you expect the company to survive, how you might exit the business—and even how hard you want to work each day. It's easy to disagree about the answers to these questions at the beginning, but it's incredibly stressful to disagree about them after the business has started to assume liabilities."

Marketing

"Most clients," said Khoi, "when they hire a design studio, take the attitude that the studio is lucky to work with them, that they selected them from a plentiful pool of design companies bidding on their business. To many clients, design studios are, in a sense, interchangeable. So if you don't want to do something the client's way, if you don't want to let them integrate their staff on your team or hand over your development files midway through a project or make certain changes to your approach, well, they can easily hire the next studio to do it exactly the way they want it done instead," he said.

"This is a deadly position for a design studio because it essentially commoditizes the studio's value. It forces the studio into a mode where it's essentially selling units of its time and not its unique creative expertise. The only solution is to upend this equation and create the circumstances under which clients instead feel fortunate that a studio is willing to work with them. It's a critical difference, because it informs every event within the relationship between the two parties.

"How do you make this happen? There's only one way," said Khoi, "and it's not to do good work, which unfortunately is the answer that many designers prefer. Good work is a core part of what makes a successful studio, to be sure, but even more important is marketing yourself—relentlessly. It's my belief that at least a third of the investment and/or revenue of any new design studio should be devoted to getting great press coverage, creating attention-getting publications, running advertisements, sponsoring events—in short, creating insatiable excitement around the very idea of the studio. The only way to do great projects on the terms that you want is to make the possibility of working with you incredibly special to a prospective client."

Saying no

"At one point during my tenure at my old studio," said Khoi, "we were talking about strategy and one of my former colleagues recounted all of the many new business opportunities then available to us—the market was doing very well—and followed that summary with a declaration that, 'We cannot afford to say no to any of them.'

"Few things struck me as so fundamentally wrong and inconsistent with my vision as that statement did," said Khoi. "Even then, what I had already learned running that business was that saying 'no' was incredibly important, that turning down bad clients and bad projects—the ones that were outside of our expertise, outside of our budget, outside of the kind of work that would make us happy—was the only way to avoid the trap of working long and hard on miserable projects. This doesn't just go for 'established' studios; due to the time, effort and opportunity cost of saying 'yes' to bad projects, I believe it's also a surefire way to make sure young studios never get to say 'yes' to good projects. In the services business," advised Khoi, "sometimes 'no' is the most powerful, effective, and beneficial tool that you have."

Chapter 20

A FUTURE WITHOUT CLIENTS

Sooner or later, the idea of self-employment without the need to deal with clients—that is, being able to generate passive income—is going to enter your head. I love working with good clients, don't get me wrong, but I chose self-employment because there's a bit of an entrepreneur in me, and who doesn't see the appeal in earning while asleep?

I was only a couple of years into my business when I began thinking of a future exit strategy. If I were starting over, I'd be planning my exit from the outset. Again, this is not because I don't like clients, but it just makes sense: You can earn even when you're not actively working, and you can devote more time to your family without needing to worry so much about money.

Paul Bailey, co-founder of London-based 1977 Design, told me of some other reasons why he chose to incorporate a passive income stream into his business:

"Frustration with clients not implementing the design or strategy as intended; a realization that as a traditional, service-based studio we would only ever be able to charge for the amount of time we could work; more exciting opportunities to develop our own brands; real ability to put our money where our mouths are, so to say. Essentially," said Paul, "we spent years telling clients how to do it and moaning when they did it wrong; now it is up to us to do it right."

Here are some ideas that you might consider.

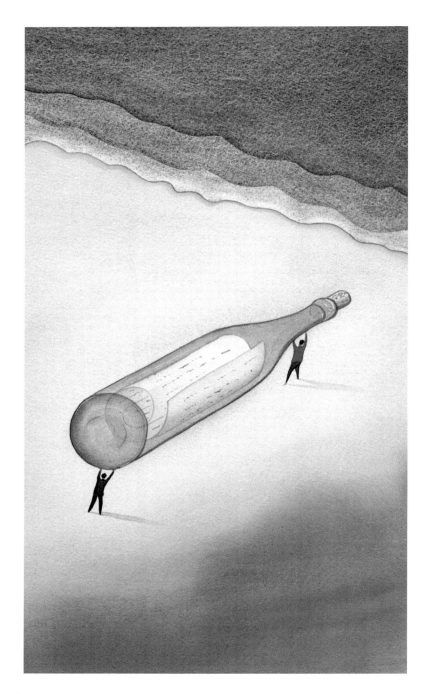

Online advertising

In chapter 10, Chris Spooner shared several ways his blog helped him throughout his time in self-employment. Nowadays, his business model has changed significantly. He picks up the story:

"The ever-increasing traffic to my online design tutorials not only brought in potential client work," said Chris, "it also began to attract more advertisers. As more banner ads were sold, a larger proportion of my monthly income was being generated from my blog, which meant I could afford to take on less client work. After all, designing for yourself is much more fun than creating work for other people! Not having to rely on a constant flow of project requests means you can be a little more picky about the projects you accept, which overall makes work more fun. The chances of landing a nightmare client are greatly reduced, and every project you work on is something you're truly excited about," he said.

"My revenue is now 100 percent made up of a mix of advertising, membership, and affiliate payments. As of late 2011, I finished off all my remaining client projects after putting up the 'Unavailable for work' sign on my websites," said Chris. "The spare time this gave me meant I could set up a little venture with my gaming channel on YouTube, which has reached the stage where it's a small revenue earner in itself."

Just like Chris, I earn advertising revenue from my blogs. I'm wary of overdoing it, however, and I limit the ad placement to a single rotating banner placed in the sidebar away from the main content. There are few things more off-putting about a website than being greeted by a raft of flashing banners and pop-ups. Additionally, if you're like me, you'll think Google AdSense looks unprofessional, so avoid it, too.

There are companies that act as the middle person between you and the advertiser: You install their code on your website, and they send you payment at the end of each month. This way, the advertiser acquisition and delivery of statistics is in their hands, so it's less work for you. These companies do, of course, take a cut of your ad revenue, but it's a hassle-free way to operate.

Alternatively, you can earn 100 percent of the ad spend by dealing directly with your advertisers. To do so, you'll need to set up a tracking system whereby you can allow the advertisers to log in and view the number of impressions, click-throughs, geographical locations, and other relevant statistics about their banner placements. If you have the time and knowledge, go for it.

Become an affiliate

As your website attracts more traffic, you have greater potential to earn money from referrals. Many Web hosts offer affiliate schemes whereby a link from your site to theirs means you get a cut of any money spent by people clicking through.

Amazon has an affiliate program known as Amazon Associates. If you link to any product sold by the company, do so through your Amazon Associate account to earn a percentage of any resulting sales. A particularly good aspect of Amazon's program is the person who clicks from your site to Amazon's doesn't need to buy the product you link to. As long as he or she makes any purchase after clicking, you'll earn commission. You can track what's bought, too, and I've found it amusing to earn money from sales of rearview mirrors, peanut butter protein bars, pink topaz necklaces, and an eye-catching green felt bowler hat.

Ship your product

We're in the service industry. We sell our time, our creativity, our passion. But that doesn't mean we can't offer a product, too.

Matt Braun and Matt Griffin are the designers at Pittsburgh-based Bearded. Matt Griffin shared the experience of how and why the duo launched Wood Type Revival onto the market:

"Because we're primarily focused on Web design and development," said Matt, "we spend the majority of our time with our faces glued to a variety of digital displays. But we're also both letterpress printers, and we *really* like wood type."

"The textures in wood type prints are lovely, the unexpected turns of the letterforms refreshing, and the vast variety of approaches delightful. Not only that, but the process of physically engaging with type is often a terrific contrast to our standard computer-tethered state.

"Once we became aware of Kickstarter," said Matt, "we immediately thought of letterpress and wondered how it might fund a wood type-related project. Over the course of a week or so, Braun kept coming to me with new project concepts, and for one reason or another they didn't feel right. Then one day he asked, 'What if we buy fonts of wood type, scan them, turn them into digital faces, and give the files back to the project funders?'

"Good ideas are like falling in love," said Matt. "When it's not the real thing, you can debate about the pros and cons forever. But when it's really right, you know it when it happens, and you'd be crazy not to act on it.

"This last idea of Braun's was one of these rare Very Good Ideas," he said. "We decided that come hell or high water, we'd launch our Kickstarter project that week. Sure, we put in some extra hours to get it done despite our client work obligations. But it didn't feel difficult because we were so excited about the concept. And that concept ultimately grew into Wood Type Revival.

"Promoting and managing the Kickstarter project was hard work. So was everything else about getting Wood Type Revival off the ground: finding type, negotiating purchases, drawing the fonts, learning new software, building the website to sell the fonts—but it always felt worth it," he said. "Every time a package of type showed up it was like designer-Christmas. Proofing each face on our press felt like some kind of Indiana Jones tomb-opening. Typing with the digital fonts for the first time? Awesome."

Wood Type Revival now provides Bearded with a passive income stream. It's relatively minor compared to the income generated by the firm's client work, but the money doesn't matter to them that much. It pays for itself, and it brings more joy into the work they do every day.

"Passive income alone is great, of course," Matt continued, "but if you can take what you're good at, and what you love, and mash them together into something useful… well, that's the real trick, isn't it?"

Other product ideas include website templates, typefaces, eBooks, and mobile apps. You could incorporate a job board onto your website whereby recruiters pay for a listing. There are many more: Brainstorm with your special talents and interests in mind.

Write a book

Creating a book requires a huge investment of time and energy, but once done, it can be sold over and over without too much additional effort. Becoming a published author doesn't just give you a passive income stream, it also gives credibility to the service you provide. Clients see that you've written a book about what they want to hire you for, and they feel more at ease about wiring you that down payment. Don't think you'll get rich from a book—especially one about design—but the extra money each month is nothing to sniff at.

You might wonder whether to team up with an established publisher or go it alone and self-publish. My advice, especially for your first book, is to pitch your idea to a publisher. The help I received when writing *Logo Design Love* proved invaluable, both from an editing viewpoint as well as for sales and marketing. Two years after publishing, it's available in ten different languages, and I'm sure I wouldn't have achieved that if it weren't for the help of my publishing team. In addition, there's a lot more credibility attached—a self-published book just doesn't command the same authority.

You can expect a publisher to pay you an advance on your royalties. This will help cover your overheads while you're unable to take on as much client work. Once your publisher recovers the advance from book sales, you'll then receive royalties at whatever commission rate you negotiated (everything's negotiable).

Although one positive of writing a book is the additional income, when you're doing the actual writing, it's very much like working with a client. You'll have chapter deadlines to keep and feedback you need to take on board.

But what's right for me isn't necessarily right for you. Thousands of people self-publish successful books, and there are more and more services available to authors for printing and distributing. So do your research and choose what you believe is the right direction.

Income as energy

Rather than calling the passive stream "income," author and designer Maggie Macnab prefers to call it "energy." She interprets all things as varying aspects of energy, with money being a human-made interpretation of energetic flow.

"At its best," Maggie said, "money facilitates community health and support for yourself and your extensions, and in the larger world it also provides a context of universal interaction between countries that can lead to healthy cultural exchange. At its worst, it becomes a vehicle to manipulate and oppress from a stance of power. My story on the subject goes like this.

"I somehow made a commitment very early on that I would only do what I loved doing and in the way I saw fit to do it," said Maggie. "To me, this only made sense: Follow your passion and you will deliver your best. I found whenever I became lax on what my soul called me to do, the results were not up to my standards and could make me very unhappy indeed. Consequently, I haven't typically had the standard benchmark for success—money—in vast reserves, but I have never lacked any of the things that support what I consider a good life: good food, consistent travel with opportunities for exploration and personal evolution, and relationships that are whole and healthy—be they with family, friends, students, or clients. I believe you create a sound life, an *integrated* life, by following what you know to be right for you. This isn't something you learn. It is something you know at your core. It leads you into creating the self you are meant to be. The world presents the experiences and relationships that we unfold through, and it is very important to participate in choosing the experiences that shape your life.

"I chose, or attracted, clients early on whose projects truly spoke to me," said Maggie. "My designs reflected that passion and were rewarded for it. They garnered recognition, enough money, and more clients. More awards got the local university's attention—the University of New Mexico/ Albuquerque—and for several years they requested that I teach logo design. For the longest time, I didn't see how I could possibly teach anyone anything and declined. I finally accepted in the mid '90s. Now teaching has become a passion. I also wrote articles, often for free, as the Internet blossomed into a massive means of communication on topics that I knew supported a good logo: symbolism, metaphor, and nature—the things I love and have always loved. This evolved into an offer for my first book, *Decoding Design: Understanding and Using Symbols in Visual Communication* (HOW Books, 2008). Out of that book, a second teaching opportunity presented itself, at Santa Fe University of Art and Design. While teaching at SFUAD, a second offer came for the next book, *Design by Nature: Using Universal Forms and Principles in Design* (New Riders, 2011). Out of this book, webinars, conferences, other teaching opportunities, and workshops are evolving. Holding to my principles has given me a true platform from which to share what I've learned as my life has unfolded through the experiences I've had," said Maggie.

"By following what I love—as a rather impassioned designer—
I have designed a life that supports who I truly am and that
has led me into my future. I offer the best I have to give to
my relationships while I strive to fulfill a life of potential. If
I might offer one bit of advice: Do what you love and be who
you are. You know it because it has always existed inside you.
There are no mistakes made in this realm, and you can't do it
wrong. Seek your own lessons in support of a life designed in
the way only you can. And don't let anyone tell you different."

These few pages only touch on the subject of passive income.
It's an area of business growth that could fill many books
over, but you'll now at least have something to think about
and plan for. It'll take a lot of time and effort at the beginning. Once in place, however, these additional revenue
streams can significantly lessen the pressure of finding new
clients and ultimately simplify your life.

Chapter 21

KEEP THE FIRE BURNING

Design is our passion, with lots of ups, but it's still a job, and like any job, there'll be downs, too. One of my "downs" is that for a number of years, I've suffered with headaches. Multiple appointments with different neurologists haven't helped, but I'm still trying various things, and I've not given up hope. Working at a computer isn't solely responsible for the pain, but I know it doesn't help, and in a company of one, it can be very difficult to drop everything at the onset of a headache in the hope it doesn't get worse.

Client deadlines are the bread and butter of what I do, and my most important client is the one I'm working with at the time. So I'll often need to work through the pain. Some occasions are more difficult than others, and at times this has led me to contemplate a profession that doesn't involve hours upon hours in front of a computer, but I just can't imagine something I'd enjoy as much as graphic design. I try to visualize myself learning a different trade: electronics, mechanics, carpentry, etc. Nothing has the same appeal, and this knowledge helps get me through the difficult days—the fact that I know I'm a designer, I know I'll always be a designer, and design is what I love.

In an effort to help you through tough spells, I asked a number of other designers what they do if a project turns out to be less exciting than they anticipated, and how they keep their passion alive through the highs and, more importantly, the inevitable lows.

Chase the opportunity, not the money

Co-founder of London-based SomeOne, Simon Manchipp, explains his simple triangular rule, which he uses to judge if a project has gone awry.

"I've never had a project go completely 'wrong,'" said Simon. "This probably has a lot to do with how I judge 'wrong.' At SomeOne, we have a simple triangular rule. 1) Do great work. 2) Have fun. 3) Make enough money to keep doing the first two things. If one of these things stops happening, the other two compensate. So abiding by this, we rarely have a huge feeling of disappointment. It's been like that for the two decades I've been in design. Chase the opportunity, not the money, and you'll generally feel good about the outcome," he said.

"For example, we did a huge project that involved travel to Italy, New Zealand, Russia, Georgia, and Italy again. It was brilliant, crazy, 24-hour fun. But we lost a vast sum of money in the end—the client did a runner—and the work wasn't amazing. However the fact that we traveled the world first-class, chartered helicopters, rode a horse bareback through Moscow, spent £5,000 on frozen rose petals, and watched a private rendition of Hamlet, in mime, on the side of a mountain, seemed to make up for the financial and creative letdowns," Simon said.

"I don't think I've ever encountered the three horsemen of the design apocalypse," he continued. "But if ever the work is crap, utterly miserable to do, and the money never appears, I'll be sure to leave the profession immediately."

Prove yourself

Partner of Netherlands-based Buro Reng, Pascal Rumph, shares what keeps him going:

"Why do graphic designers work for clients who are not as creative, and do not share the love for a well-thought-out proposal? It's not always a bed of roses," said Pascal, "but it is certainly not a burden. Without friction, there's no shine.

"We have a learning attitude," explained Pascal. "Every assignment is an opportunity to encounter new people, other thoughts, other disciplines and organizations. Asking questions, researching, analyzing, and asking more questions retrieves the unique in every assignment. That is what we love to do. Sometimes, you get little room to maneuver. Then it is especially important to do our job; guiding clients through a creative process, to show how it can be done. In the long term," said Pascal, "the chance to prove ourselves is priceless. That's what keeps us going."

First with who, then what

Thierry Brunfaut, partner and head of creation at Base, lays down some pointers that help him stay focused.

"As a young designer, for years, you design for the sake of design. You design for 'the what,' the outcome: the logo, the poster, the book. But one day," said Thierry, "you realize that's not the most important thing. The most important thing is: 'with who.'

"Select carefully the people you are working with, above any other consideration. Your team. Your collaborators. Your clients. If you like them, if you can openly dialog with them, all your design projects will be challenging, interesting, and fun," he said. "That's my only advice in design practice: first with who, then what."

"I've made a ten-point list of criteria to help the Base teams to communicate and design better:

1. Each job has a context. We study it before we start.

2. First, concept. Then, design.

3. We don't design for designers. We design for people.

4. Every item we produce is a communication tool.

5. We challenge design habits and media. We play with codes.

6. If it looks familiar, we will try something else.

7. We freely mix our creative disciplines.

8. We try and fail. We are not afraid to make mistakes.

9. We believe there is no bad taste or good taste.

10. We surprise. We want people to smile."

Create what others can't imagine

Austin-based Armin Vit of UnderConsideration gets through those unexciting projects by knowing that he will, at the very least, get paid.

"Many designers will tell you that you have to be heroic and give every client your all and never quit," said Armin. "That's a load of crap. Some clients and some projects don't deserve your 100 percent, for whatever reason, and sometimes what keeps you going is knowing that the project will eventually end, you will cash your check, and avoid the client or another project like it again. I wish there was something more uplifting and cheerleader-ish I could say," added Armin, "but sometimes there is no real light at the end of the tunnel. You just hope to make it to the other end, even if it's the middle of the night and there is no light. At least you'll be out."

Armin's reasons for loving design *are* more uplifting.

"It never ceases to amaze me," he said. "There is always someone doing something that I never imagined could be done that way. Since I am constantly reporting [on the site Brand-New] on what the industry does, I love seeing it evolve and finding new ways to engage with audiences. I love that it's so diverse and so broad and that there are dozens of answers for the same problem."

Focus on the right projects for you

Blair Thomson, creative director at Believe in, a design studio in Exeter, England, gives some balanced advice for surviving those tough projects.

"Take a deep breath," said Blair. "Put your head down, and get on with it. We all have projects that defeated our expectations. The same goes for clients—about designers. There are usually good reasons for this, but at the end of the day it is your duty to complete the work to the best of your abilities. If the client is making things impossible and you've done everything you can to work with his or her demands and feedback, terminate the contract and leave it behind," advises Blair. "This will take great courage but strengthens confidence and allows you to focus your efforts on the right projects and clients for you. The best relationships—of any kind—are those based on trust and respect."

Blair keeps his mind tuned and sharp a number of ways.

"First, and most important," he said, "I ensure I have some time in the day away from the desk—some non-computer time. Some non-studio time, in fact. Fresh air and a moment of peace away from the buzz of work for a short while recharges and opens up the mind. A walk, a cycle, a sit down in the park, or a coffee and a bite to eat are all good examples. Making a bit of time away from things, in the end, equates to more productive time where it counts—in the studio.

"I also collect stuff: old books, posters, stamps, packaging, old type specimens, old technology, paraphernalia of all types.

"There is always something inspirational from the past that brings out a new idea," he explained. "I have a bit of a fascination with the modernist era. Only looking at the 'now'—blogs, visual curation sites, agency showcases, etc.—risks mere cloning and unoriginal ideas.

"Talk more with your client and her audience," advises Blair. "Greater understanding and insight into the brief, the brand, the stakeholder, and objectives of the project help produce far stronger and much more relevant output. More than ever, effective measures are expected of your work, so invest some time beyond the design itself."

Take control

Paul Buck, director of London-based Zerofee, found his professional cure by leaving employment to form his own studio.

"After finishing my degree and finding employment within a design studio," said Paul, "I became rapidly disillusioned with the kind of projects and clients I handled. In my experience, a lack of personal control over the agency and its ethical stance leads to unprofessional conduct and demoralizing work, aesthetically and philosophically. Forming Zerofee cured that. There's no going back."

Use the bad to appreciate the good

Luke Tonge, a graphic designer based in Birmingham, England, knows that in order to truly value your best clients, it's necessary to work with those who aren't so ideal.

"It's rare," said Luke, "that a project doesn't become somehow compromised as it progresses from idea to execution—constraints, financial limitations, unwanted external input, and so on—but I find that when I take a step back and re-adjust my perspective, each project can be appreciated as a learning experience. I've gleaned more long-term value from the most difficult projects than the quick wins. Plus, everyone needs a good war-story or two," he said, "and it helps you to really appreciate the good clients."

Luke also warns against relying on praise from peers to keep you motivated.

"As soon as you fall into the trap of needing acclaim or recognition for your work," he said, "you become hostage to it. If, however, your reward comes from knowing you've done the best you can, or you've effected a change in some way or moved an audience, it's much easier to protect your ego and feel genuinely satisfied."

Rise above it

When asked how he recovers from the lows, David Hyde of Studio Hyde chose this appropriate quote:

"In the words of Mahatma Gandhi, 'Remember that there is always a limit to self-indulgence but none to self-restraint, and let us daily progress in that direction.' Your low points are, after all is said and done, your self-indulgence. Rise above them," he said.

Jump in with both feet

Chris Harman, CEO and creative director at Parent Design in Bournemouth, England, finds something exciting in any project he accepts.

"We're very careful who we work with at Parent and don't take on anything we don't believe in," said Chris. "The thought is that to give a client and a project their best, you need to be fully behind them with both feet. If not, the project will never be as good as it could be. Hopefully, making the right choices in the first place avoids issues, but if issues do arise, just look at it from a different angle for a while."

Pay your dues

Karen Huang, creative director of Manic Design in Singapore, understands that it's all part of your progression when projects don't go quite according to plan.

"When a project goes what I call 'pear-shaped,'" she said, "I often force myself to look back on similarly disastrous projects and remind myself how they eventually led to or attracted the type of work that I wanted.

"The key is to see it as strategic portfolio building or paying your dues or delayed gratification—whatever you call it. It then becomes very palatable," she says. "By seeing it as a stepping-stone to attracting the type of work I want, things get much better. This is known by psychologists as cognitive reframing.

"Suddenly working with a logo designed by the CEO's son is all-in-a-day's-work. Working with the proverbial 'stupid clients' just makes for more interesting war stories."

Make something beautiful

Bob Mytton, partner and creative director at Mytton Williams in Bath, England, talks about his motivations.

"Seeing and being constantly reminded of the power of design [is inspiring], whether it be changing perceptions, helping make something easier to understand, or just making something beautiful," says Bob. "It could be discussing new creative possibilities with the team in the studio, seeing great work by other designers, or just speaking to clients about the results from a recent branding project."

Be deeply satisfied

Cristian Paul, founding partner of Bucharest-based Brandient, reminds us of the long-lasting rewards we reap from our endeavors.

"Let's be honest," said Cristian. "Design must be one of the least boring career options available on the labor market. It might be at moments—for the most competitive ones—a despairing, OCD-inducing affair, but what passion isn't maddening at times?" he asked.

"A design career comes with an extensive set of gratification mechanisms, but the most important ones I think are very subtle: the slow, minute accumulation of work and the inspiration emerging from teamwork.

"I'll explain the first by comparing design to advertising," he said. "In advertising there is a distance of weeks between a brief coming in and the final product out there on the billboards and the TV screens—very fast, almost a rush of instant gratification. Then, in weeks, the work reaches its preprogrammed end-of-life and it vanishes without a trace. Gone.

"In design," Cristian explains, "projects are long—some take more than one year to conceptualize and even longer to get produced. Then gradually they turn up on the shelves of the stores, above the entrance of the buildings or on top of them, on the Web, on vehicle livery, on shopping bags and flags and your favorite team's sports equipment. It just slowly builds and builds, and it never seems to stop. You look around wherever you go and see your work growing—a life well spent. Not a quick satisfaction, but a very deep one. A mature one."

Be part of the community

"I don't find it at all difficult to stay motivated about the Web," reflects California-based Chris Coyier of CSS Tricks. "There are so many people doing so much great stuff right now who are *also* happily sharing the why and how they did it—it's just incredible," he said. "I feed off others, work and contribute back all I can. When you feel like you are part of a community, even if you're working on your own individual projects, staying motivated is easy."

Have pride

Ryan Tym of London-based Unreal is motivated by three things: pride, jealousy, and people.

"A desire to produce work that I and those close to me are proud of. A jealously of peers and industry figures who create work I wish I'd done for projects I wish I'd had. And lastly, being surrounded by a team of people who creatively challenge and better each other on a daily basis," said Ryan.

"The jealousy and the people always ensure my passion for the job stays fresh and that in turn helps to build the pride. Thankfully, the pace of the work these days means that if one project doesn't quite turn out as planned, there's always another one just around the corner to refocus on. In that respect, even the clients help to keep the job fresh."

Step away from the specifics

Matt McInerney, a designer at Pentagram in New York, finds his inspiration by discovering the underlying ideas in the world around us.

"Finding your inspiration is key," he says. "As time goes on, I find less and less inspiration in pages filled with posters or endless grids of images out of context. Instead, I turn to sources that aren't so heavily stamped with the design label. Stepping away from the specifics of your work and discovering the underlying ideas, the secret points of inspiration, and the often overlooked systems of our built environment and experiences can be refreshing and motivating in a deeper way."

Let others motivate you

Associate creative director at New York-based AKQA, Antonio Carusone, does two things to stay fresh.

"I subscribe to a ton of design blogs," said Antonio. "This allows me to see what is being produced outside of my little world and also keeps me motivated. Additionally, I always try to design, even if it's a made-up project. For example, if I want to learn something new in HTML5, I'll design and code a little site for myself."

"Some projects aren't so exciting, but it's still important to identify and focus on the problem, then try to solve it. For instance, I recently had to design a boring email that was all text, but the email carried an important message, so we focused on making sure the message was clear and concise, and that the design didn't get in the way."

Give and take

Portland-based designer Shauna Haider talks about the need to be flexible when dealing with clients.

"I'm aware that not every project is going to be amazing in my eyes," said Shauna. "But what matters most to me is that my client is satisfied with the outcome. I'm always striving to meet that middle ground so that we're both happy, but design is definitely a profession rife with give and take."

Shauna added, "I continue on every day because I truly love what I do. Through the good and the bad, design still feels like the right fit and I feel incredibly lucky that I am able to follow my professional calling."

Work on side projects

London-based Web designer and developer Daniel Howells shares how small side projects can teach and inspire.

"Having side projects is extremely important for me," said Daniel. "They are spaces in which to experiment with new techniques and fail without getting hurt. And I find it humbling that the side projects tend to be what get me new client work. It's sometimes hard to find the time to fit them all in, but in the long run it helps a great deal with motivation," he said.

Perhaps my own side projects, such as the sites Logo Design Love and Identity Designed, are the reason why you're reading this book, because without those websites, my publisher would never have approached me. It's funny where these things lead.

Graphic designer Emily Kane, also based in London, agrees.

"I retain creative satisfaction," said Emily "by balancing client work with self-initiated projects and indulging in traditional drawing practice and artwork creation to my own briefs. This helps the creative juices flow and benefits my mental approach to client work."

On the topic of motivations, I asked Daniel Howells to share what keeps him in the profession.

"A big part of what I do," said Daniel "is showcase work by other designers, on siteInspire and Creative Journal. Through those two websites, I know that regardless of how well or poorly I regard my own skills and work, there is *always* somebody else doing better, more astonishing work to aspire to. Everyone should always keep that in the back of his or her mind," he advised.

"And when the going gets tough with bad clients or disappointing work, as an independent it's always worth remembering that we're very lucky to be in the position we are: doing what we love with the freedom and flexibility the profession provides."

Well said.

Love what you do

Let's say our lives span a maximum of 100 years. If 33 years are taken up with sleep, 10 years in childhood, and 20 years lost in old age, that leaves just 37 years to create something meaningful. Don't waste that time with sorrow, complaints, or unnecessary negativity. We create our best work when we're in a positive frame of mind. We have no idea if, after death, we'll ever experience anything again, so most importantly, enjoy your profession, appreciate your surroundings, and love using design to make things better.

Chapter 22

RESOURCES

I've purposely kept this roundup of recommended reads and resources brief because the preceding chapters should have given you plenty of ideas on how to outwit your competitors. That said, you'll find a broader selection hyperlinked on the resources page of my book's website.

www.workformoneydesignforlove.com

Books

It's Not How Good You Are, It's How Good You Want To Be, by Paul Arden (Phaidon, 2003)

How to Win Friends and Influence People, by Dale Carnegie (Simon & Schuster, reissue edition, 2009)

Design is a Job, by Mike Monteiro (A Book Apart, 2012)

Steal Like an Artist, by Austin Kleon (Workman, 2012)

The Win Without Pitching Manifesto, by Blair Enns (Rockbench, 2010)

Designing Brand Identity, by Alina Wheeler (Wiley, 2009)

Word of Mouth Marketing, by Andy Sernovitz (Greenleaf, 2012)

100 Things Every Designer Needs to Know About People, by Susan Weinschenk (New Riders, 2011)

Don't Make Me Think, by Steve Krug (New Riders, 2005)

How to Be a Graphic Designer without Losing Your Soul, by Adrian Shaughnessy (Princeton Architectural Press, 2010)

How to Think Like a Great Graphic Designer, by Debbie Millman (Allworth Press, 2011)

The $100 Startup, by Chris Guillebeau (Crown Business, 2012)

Made to Stick, by Chip Heath and Dan Heath (Random House, 2007)

Lateral Thinking, by Edward de Bono (Harper Colophon, 1973)

Talent is Not Enough, by Shel Perkins (New Riders, 2010)

The Designer's Guide to Marketing and Pricing, by Ilise Benun and Peleg Top (HOW Books, 2008)

101 Contrarian Ideas About Advertising, by Bob Hoffman (Hoffman/Lews, 2012)

Aesop's Fables, by Aesop (Chronicle Books, 2000)

Logo Design Love, by me (New Riders, 2010)

Blogs

Seth's Blog, by Seth Godin

CR Blog, by Creative Review

Zen Habits, by Leo Babauta

the johnson banks thought for the week, by johnson banks

Subtraction, by Khoi Vinh

ideasonideas, by Eric Karjaluoto

Identity Designed, and Logo Design Love, by me

Publishers

(For your book pitch.)

Peachpit

HOW Books

Rockport

Laurence King

Wiley

Workman

Print

Self-publishing

(Options if you don't want to work with an established publisher.)

CreateSpace

Lulu

Blurb

Xlibris

Ad providers

(Companies that pay you to display ads from relevant third parties.)

The Deck

Fusion Ads

Carbon

AdPacks

InfluAds

Project help

(A few resources to help with your client projects.)

WeTransfer (for sending files of up to 2GB)

Inker Linker (for finding recommended print companies)

Lovely as a Tree (on being more environmentally aware)

Don't forget

Find these and many more helpful links on the resources page of the website.

www.workformoneydesignforlove.com

Contributors

Adam Ladd	www.ladd-design.com	(chapter 11)
Alina Wheeler	www.alinawheeler.com	(chapters 15, 16, 19)
Andrea Austoni	www.andreaaustoni.com	(chapters 13, 16)
Andrew Kelsall	www.andrewkelsall.com	(chapter 11)
Antoinette Marie Johnson	www.atmediadesign.com	(chapter 11)
Antonio Carusone	www.aisleone.net	(chapter 21)
Armin Vit	www.underconsideration.com	(chapter 21)
Atakan Seckin	www.aseckin.com	(chapter 18)
Bernadette Jiwa	www.thestoryoftelling.com	(chapter 7)
Blair Thomson	www.believein.co.uk	(chapter 21)
Bob Mytton	www.myttonwilliams.co.uk	(chapter 21)
Chris Coyier	www.chriscoyier.net	(chapter 21)
Chris Harman	www.parentdesign.co.uk	(chapter 21)
Chris Spooner	www.chrisspooner.com	(chapters 10, 20)
Con Kennedy	www.conkennedy.ie	(chapter 1)
Cristian Paul	www.brandient.com	(chapter 21)
Daniel Howells	www.howells.ws	(chapter 21)
Darragh Neely	www.darraghneely.com	(chapter 14)
David Hyde	www.davidthedesigner.com	(chapter 21)
Emily Kane	www.emilykane.co.uk	(chapter 21)
Eric Karjaluoto	www.erickarjaluoto.com	(chapters 12, 18)
Fiona Burrage	www.theclickdesign.com	(chapter 14)
Gary Holmes	www.gariphic.com	(chapter 11)
Ian Vadas	www.ianvadas.com	(chapter 17)
Ivan Chermayeff	www.cgstudionyc.com	(chapters 16, 18, 19)
Jenny Theolin	www.jennytheolin.com	(chapter 11)
Jerry Kuyper	www.jerrykuyper.com	(chapters 18, 19)
Jessica Hagy	www.jessicahagy.info	(chapter 19)
John Clifford	www.thinkstudionyc.com	(chapter 18)
Jonathan Selikoff	www.selikoffco.com	(chapter 17)
JP Jones	www.paige1media.com	(chapter 13)
Karen Huang	www.wearemanic.com	(chapter 21)
Karishma Kasabia	www.kishandco.co	(chapters 11, 16)
Katherine Ramsland	www.katherineramsland.com	(chapter 8)
Khoi Vinh	www.subtraction.com	(chapter 19)
Lee Newham	www.designedbygoodpeople.com	(chapters 11, 12)
Lita Mikrut	www.litamikrut.com	(chapter 11)
Liza Lowinger	www.aptone.com	(chapter 13)

Luke Mysse	www.crossgrain.com	(chapter 9)
Luke Tonge	www.luketonge.com	(chapter 21)
Maggie Macnab	www.macnabdesign.com	(chapter 20)
Mark Bloom	www.mashcreative.co.uk	(chapter 11)
Matt Griffin	www.bearded.com	(chapter 20)
Matt McInerney	www.matt.cc	(chapter 21)
Meredith Gossland	www.lbgba.org	(chapter 9)
Mike Dempsey	www.studiodempsey.co.uk	(chapter 19)
Mike Reed	www.reedwords.co.uk	(chapter 16)
Nancy Wu	www.nancywudesign.com	(chapter 16)
Nick Asbury	www.nickasbury.com	(chapter 18)
Pascal Rumph	www.buroreng.nl	(chapter 21)
Patricia Schaefer	www.contemporary-native.com	(chapter 17)
Paul Buck	www.zerofee.org	(chapter 21)
Phil Cook	www.matdolphin.com	(chapters 9, 11)
Reese Spykerman	www.designbyreese.com	(chapter 19)
Russell Holmes	www.icodesign.co.uk	(chapter 14)
Ryan Tym	www.ryantym.com	(chapter 21)
Shauna Haider	www.nubbytwiglet.com	(chapter 21)
Sheena Oosten	www.sheenaoosten.com	(chapter 14)
Simon Manchipp	www.someoneinlondon.com	(chapter 21)
Stellan Johansson	www.weare1910.com	(chapter 11)
Steven Key	www.keycreate.co.uk	(chapter 11)
Suzana Shash	www.suzanashash.com	(chapter 11)
Ted Leonhardt	www.tedleonhardt.com	(chapter 16)
Thierry Brunfaut	www.basedesign.com	(chapter 21)
Tim Lapetino	www.hexanine.com	(chapter 14)
Tom Actman	www.matdolphin.com	(chapters 9, 11)
Von Glitschka	www.vonglitschka.com	(chapter 17)

Thank you.

I'm more grateful than you know.

INDEX

WATCH
READ
CREATE

Unlimited online access to all Peachpit, Adobe Press, Apple Training and New Riders videos and books, as well as content from other leading publishers including: O'Reilly Media, Focal Press, Sams, Que, Total Training, John Wiley & Sons, Course Technology PTR, Class on Demand, VTC and more.

No time commitment or contract required! Sign up for one month or a year. All for $19.99 a month

SIGN UP TODAY
peachpit.com/creativeedge